The Clinical Lacan

THE LACANIAN CLINICAL FIELD

A series of books edited by
Judith Feher Gurewich, Ph.D.
in collaboration with
Susan Fairfield

The Clinical Lacan

Joël Dor

EDITED BY
Judith Feher Gurewich, Ph.D.
IN COLLABORATION WITH
Susan Fairfield

JASON ARONSON INC.
Northvale, New Jersey
London

This work, published as part of the program of aid for publication, received support from the Ministry of Foreign Affairs of the Cultural Service of the French Embassy in the United States. *Cet ouvrage publié dans le cadre du programme d'aide à la publication bénéficie du soutien du Ministère des Affaires Etrangères du Service Culturel de l'Ambassade de France représenté aux Etats-Unis.*

Production Editor: Elaine Lindenblatt

This book was set in 11 pt. Berkeley by Alpha Graphics of Pittsfield, NH and printed and bound by Integrated Book Technology of Troy, NY.

Library of Congress Cataloging-in-Publication Data
Dor, Joël.
    [Structures et clinique psychanalytique. English]
    The clinical Lacan / by Joël Dor : edited by Judith Feher Gurewich in collaboration with Susan Fairfield.
      p. cm — (The Lacanian clinical field)
    Companion v. to: Introduction to the reading of Lacan.
    Includes bibliographical references and index.
    ISBN 0-7657-0042-5
    1. Psychoanalysis. 2. Lacan, Jacques, 1901–   . 3. Psychology, Pathological. 4. Subjectivity. I. Gurewich, Judith Feher.
II. Dor, Joël. Introduction à la lecture de Lacan. English.
III. Title. IV. Series.
    [DNLM: 1. Lacan, Jacques, 1901–   . 2. Psychology Theory.
WM 460 D693s 1997a]
RC506.D6513 1997
616.89'17—dc20
DNLM/DLC
for Library of Congress   96-32060

Printed in the United States of America on acid-free paper. For information and catalog write to Jason Aronson Inc., 230 Livingston Street, Northvale, New Jersey 07647-1731. Or visit our website: http://www.aronson.com

Contents

III: THE HYSTERICAL STRUCTURE

IV: THE OBSESSIONAL STRUCTURE

The Lacanian Clinical Field:
Series Overview

Lacanian psychoanalysis exists, and the new series, The Lacanian Clinical Field, is here to prove it. The clinical expertise of French practitioners deeply influenced by the thought of Jacques Lacan has finally found a publishing home in the United States. Books that have been acclaimed in France, Italy, Spain, Greece, South America, and Japan for their clarity, didactic power, and clinical relevance will now be at the disposal of the American psychotherapeutic and academic communities. These books cover a range of topics, including theoretical introductions; clinical approaches to neurosis, perversion and psychosis; child psychoanalysis; conceptualizations of femininity; psychoanalytic readings of American literature; and more. Thus far nine books are in preparation.

Though all these works are clinically relevant, they will also be of great interest to those American scholars who have taught and used Lacan's theories for over a decade. What better opportunity for the academic world of literary criticism, philosophy, human sciences, women's studies, film studies, and multicultural

studies finally to have access to the clinical insights of a theorist
known primarily for his revolutionary vision of the formation
of the human subject. Thus The Lacanian Clinical Field goes
beyond introducing the American clinician to a different psychoanalytic outlook. It brings together two communities that have
grown progressively estranged from each other. For indeed, the
time when the Frankfurt School, Lionel Trilling, Erich Fromm,
Herbert Marcuse, Philip Rieff and others were fostering exchanges between the academic and the psychoanalytic communities is gone, and in the process psychoanalysis has lost some
of its vibrancy.

The very limited success of ego psychology in bringing psychoanalysis into the domain of science has left psychoanalysis in
need of a metapsychology that is able not only to withstand the
pernicious challenges of psychopharmacology and psychiatry but
also to accommodate the findings of cognitive and developmen-
tal psychology. Infant research has put many of Freud's insights
into question, and the attempts to replace a one-body psychology with a more interpersonal or intersubjective approach have
led to dissension within the psychoanalytic community. Many
theorists are of the opinion that the road toward scientific legiti-
macy requires a certain allegiance with Freud's detractors, who
are convinced that the unconscious and its sexual underpinnings
are merely an aberration. Psychoanalysis continues to be prac-
ticed, however, and according to both patients and analysts the
uncovering of unconscious motivations continues to provide a
sense of relief. But while there has been a burgeoning of different
psychoanalytic schools of thought since the desacralization of
Freud, no theoretical agreement has been reached as to why such
relief occurs.

Nowadays it can sometimes seem that Freud is read much
more scrupulously by literary critics and social scientists than

by psychoanalysts. This is not entirely a coincidence. While the psychoanalytic community is searching for a new metapsychology, the human sciences have acquired a level of theoretical sophistication and complexity that has enabled them to read Freud under a new lens. Structural linguistics and structural anthropology have transformed conventional appraisals of human subjectivity and have given Freud's unconscious a new status. Lacan's teachings, along with the works of Foucault and Derrida, have been largely responsible for the explosion of new ideas that have enhanced the interdisciplinary movement pervasive in academia today.

The downside of this remarkable intellectual revolution, as far as psychoanalysis is concerned, is the fact that Lacan's contribution has been derailed from its original trajectory. No longer perceived as a theory meant to enlighten the practice of psychoanalysis, his brilliant formulations have been both adapted and criticized so as to conform to the needs of purely intellectual endeavors far removed from clinical reality. This state of affairs is certainly in part responsible for Lacan's dismissal by the psychoanalytic community. Moreover, Lacan's "impossible" style has been seen as yet another proof of the culture of obscurantism that French intellectuals seem so fond of.

In this context the works included in The Lacanian Clinical Field should serve as an eye-opener at both ends of the spectrum. The authors in the series are primarily clinicians eager to offer to professionals in psychoanalysis, psychiatry, psychology, and other mental-health disciplines a clear and succinct didactic view of Lacan's work. Their goal is not so much to emphasize the radically new insights of the Lacanian theory of subjectivity and its place in the history of human sciences as it is to show how this difficult and complex body of ideas can enhance clinical work. Therefore, while the American clinician will be made aware that Lacanian psychoanalysis is not primarily a staple of literary criticism or philosophy but a praxis meant to cure patients of their psychic distress, the academic community will be exposed for the first time to a reading of Lacan that is in sharp contrast with the literature that has thus far informed them about his theory. In that sense Lacan's teachings return to the clinical reality to which they primarily belong.

Moreover, the clinical approach of the books in this series will shed a new light on the critical amendments that literary scholars and feminist theoreticians have brought to Lacan's conceptualization of subjectivity. While Lacan has been applauded for having offered an alternative to Freud's biological determinism, he has also been accused of nevertheless remaining phallocentric in his formulation of sexual difference. Yet this criticism, one that may be valid outside of the clinical reality—psychoanalysis is both an ingredient and an effect of culture—may not have the same relevance in the clinical context. For psychoanalysis as a praxis has a radically different function from the one it currently serves in academic discourse. In the latter, psychoanalysis is perceived both as an ideology fostering patriarchal beliefs and as a theoretical tool for constructing a vision of the subject no longer dependent on a phallocratic system. In the former, however, the issue of phallocracy loses its political impact. Psychoanalytic practice can only retroactively unravel the ways in which the patient's psychic life has been constituted, and in that sense it can only reveal the function the phallus plays in the psychic elaboration of sexual difference.

The Lacanian Clinical Field, therefore, aims to undo certain prejudices that have affected Lacan's reputation up to now in both the academic and the psychoanalytic communities. While these prejudices stem from rather different causes—Lacan is perceived as too patriarchal and reactionary in the one and too far removed from clinical reality in the other—they both seem to overlook the fact that the fifty years that cover the period of Lacan's teachings were mainly devoted to working and reworking the meaning and function of psychoanalysis, not necessarily as a science or even as a human science, but as a practice that can nonetheless rely on a solid and coherent metapsychology. This double debunking of received notions may not only enlarge the respective frames of reference of both the therapeutic and the academic communities; it may also allow them to find a common denominator in a metapsychology that has derived its "scientific" status from the unexpected realm of the humanities.

I would like to end this overview to the series as a whole with a word of warning and a word of reassurance. One of the great difficulties for an American analyst trying to figure out the Lacanian "genre" is the way these clinical theorists explain their theoretical point of view as if it were coming straight from Freud. Yet Lacan's Freud and the American Freud are far from being transparent to each other. Lacan dismantled the Freudian corpus and rebuilt it on entirely new foundations, so that the new edifice no longer resembled the old. At the same time he always downplayed, with a certain *coquetterie*, his position as a theory builder, because he was intent on proving that despite all odds he had remained true to Freud's deepest insights. Since Lacan was very insistent on keeping Freudian concepts as the raw material of his theory, Lacanian analysts of the second generation have followed in their master's footsteps and have continued to read Freud scrupulously in order to expand, with new insights, this large structure that had been laid out. Moreover, complicated historical circumstances have fostered their isolation, so that their acquaintance with recent psychoanalytic developments outside of France has been limited. Lacan's critical views on ego psychology and selected aspects of object relations theory have continued to inform their vision of American psychoanalysis and have left them unaware that certain of their misgivings about these schools of thought are shared by some of their colleagues in the United States. This apparently undying allegiance to Freud, therefore, does not necessarily mean that Lacanians have not moved beyond him, but rather that their approach is different from that of their American counterparts. While the latter often tend to situate their work as a reaction to Freud, the Lacanian strategy always consists in rescuing Freud's insights and resituating them in a context free of biological determinism.

Second, I want to repeat that the expository style of the books of this series bears no resemblance to Lacan's own writings. Lacan felt that Freud's clarity and didactic talent had ultimately led to distortions and oversimplifications, so that his own notoriously "impossible" style was meant to serve as a metaphor for the difficulty of listening to the unconscious. Cracking his difficult writings involves not only readers' intellectual effort but also their unconscious processes; comprehension will dawn as reader-analysts recognize in their own work what was expressed in sibylline fashion in the text. Some of Lacan's followers continued this tradition, fearing that clear exposition would leave no room for the active participation of the reader. Others felt strongly that although Lacan's point was well taken it was not necessary to prolong indefinitely an ideology of obscurantism liable to fall into the same traps as the ones Lacan was denouncing in the first place. Such a conviction was precisely what made this series, The Lacanian Clinical Field, possible.

—Judith Feher Gurewich, Ph.D.

Editor's Preface

JUDITH FEHER GUREWICH

It is unquestionable that Dor's *Introduction to the Reading of Lacan* is an efficient book that systematically and forcefully presents the architectonics of Lacan's theory. However, the need of the American clinician to understand what a Lacanian analyst actually does in his practice is not addressed in Lacan's complex work. To fill this gap *The Clinical Lacan* is offered as a companion text to the *Introduction*. Consisting of Joël Dor's lectures to psychoanalysts in training, this manual is centered on the diagnosis of psychic structure and thus provides immediate access to the landmarks that guide Lacanian psychoanalytic practice.

The concept of psychic structure (which, according to Freud, distinguishes neurosis, psychosis, and the perversions) is seminal in Lacan's theory. With the help of exciting clinical examples, Dor explains the crucial difference between symptoms—that is, what can be phenomenologically grasped—and the actual psychic structure of the subject, a structure that can be revealed only through the discourse of the patient in the psychoanalytic situation. Such a structure refers to a specific mode of desiring, and, although this mode of desiring takes on multiple shapes and forms, an attentive clinician will eventually be able to distinguish an hysteric from an obsessional or a pervert from a psychotic.

Yet here again *The Clinical Lacan* is not a book directed exclusively to clinicians. Anyone interested in psychoanalysis, and not only academicians, will find in these clinical descriptions much food for thought. Dor makes it clear that pathology and subjectivity are tightly interwoven, so that readers themselves may feel implicated in the text as they wonder which psychic structure is their own. According to Dor, each of us is situated in our intersubjective world with a specific way of desiring and wanting to be desired. What this book reveals is that we spend most of our lives unwittingly working out the metaphysical meaning of sexual difference. *The Clinical Lacan* is faithful to the ethics of psychoanalysis in that it rigorously distinguishes its field from that of social reality. What psychoanalysis discovers is the intersubjective reality of the unconscious, the dynamics that operate "behind our backs." Thus, in Dor's text, fetishism, transsexualism, tranvestism, hysteria, and obsessional neurosis are never presented as deviations from a norm but rather as specific modes of desiring and constituting one's subjectivity.

In this sense, *The Clinical Lacan* constitutes a challenge to the recent attempt of American psychoanalysis and psychiatry to revise the diagnostic nosography of sexual orientations and practices so as to accommodate to the climate of "political correctness." This challenge is twofold. First, the book reveals by way of contrast how far American psychoanalysis has moved from the Freudian field to a more phenomenological approach. For by conceptualizing the new clinical categories of borderline and narcissistic disorders in terms of certain modes of behavior and certain types of personality, American psychoanalysis neglects unconscious motivations as they are manifested in the patient's discourse. Second, once the American analyst realizes that these Freudian psychic structures, as reformulated by Lacanian theory, merely map out the various paths that human desire may follow, he or she may wonder whether hysteria, obsessional neurosis, and the perversions are indeed dying species.

The Clinical Lacan, then, is a companion to *Introduction to the Reading of Lacan* in the sense that it defines how theory can be brought to the reality of the psychoanalytic situation. First in its genre, this manual sets the tone for the other books in the series, whose common aim is precisely to bring life and practical usefulness to a psychoanalytic movement that has been so long misperceived in this country as overintellectualized and divorced from the daily vicissitudes of analytic work.

Introduction

JOËL DOR

I'd like to explain some of the reasons that led me to write on the topic of psychic structures and clinical psychoanalysis. First of all, this is a synthetic approach to psychoanalysis, organized around the notion of diagnosis. But the issue of diagnosis immediately brings us, as clinicians, to what might be called a technical dilemma in the field of the unconscious, as soon as we are confronted—in the urgency we know so well—with the vicissitudes of practice. The problem is the difficulty in finding landmarks, points of reference. We regularly encounter certain confusions with regard to clinical reference points, if any exist at all.

There is no way to avoid this difficulty entirely. It is largely a matter of taking the time to acquire clinical experience and of having the right subjective tools with which to tackle clinical problems. When it comes to these two factors, no teaching can take the place of the psychic work they require. But we can still "mark out the ground." This expression is metaphorical, but it addresses the need for rigorous clinical guidelines. Even if these guidelines in no way preempt the relevance of clinical practice, they are, nonetheless, metapsychological landmarks that allow us to define certain stable nosological entities to the extent that this nosology is consistently placed in its underlying context: the investigation of the unconscious.

These metapsychological landmarks are of two kinds. First, there are those that are likely to appear in the process of formulating the diagnosis (the diagnosis, that is, in the very specific psychoanalytic sense). Second, we must adhere to guidelines pertaining to the conduct of the treatment and to its dynamics. Strictly speaking, therefore, these reference points are not transmittable outside the work each of us does in examining his or her individual practice. Thus it goes without saying that in this book I shall not be trying to convey them in an exhaustive manner. My task, instead, is to introduce the concept of diagnosis from a structural perspective, that is, a perspective based on the dynamic and economic profile of the main psychopathological structures: the perverse, the hysterical, and the obsessional.[1]

---

[1] I have omitted the psychotic structures not only because of their complexity but also because of the limited time available for the series of lectures (in Rio de Janeiro, 1990) that formed the basis of this study.

Part I

Diagnosis and Structure

The Concept of Diagnosis in Psychoanalysis[1]

Let us begin looking at the problem of diagnosis in the field of psychopathology by considering some of Freud's ideas on this matter. Early on, in 1895—that is, right from the beginning of psychoanalysis—he speaks of the technical difficulties he encountered in applying Breuer's therapeutic method of detection and abreaction in treating hysteria, and he draws several important conclusions (Freud and Breuer 1895). He notes, on the one hand, that he finds it hard to have a clear idea about a case of neurosis without having analyzed it in depth. But, on the other hand, he adds that before we can grasp the case in detail we need to establish a diagnosis in order to determine the orientation of the treatment. In other words, right at the outset of his work Freud pinpointed the ambiguity surrounding the problem of diagnosis in clinical psychoanalysis: the need to formulate a diagnosis prematurely in order to decide on the course of treatment, even

---

1. For a more detailed discussion of this topic, see Dor 1987 (forthcoming in translation from Jason Aronson Inc.).

though the relevance of such a diagnosis will be confirmed only after the treatment has been under way for some time.

This paradox is what makes psychoanalytic diagnosis unique. We need to clarify this notion and put it in perspective by comparing it to the concept of diagnosis in the medical field. A medical diagnosis is set in motion by two criteria. First, there is the criterion of observation, aimed at determining the nature of a complaint or an illness on the basis of a fixed system of meanings, and then there is the criterion of classification, which permits the detection of a given pathological state within the framework of a nosography. Thus medical diagnosis always takes place from a twofold perspective, referring as it does both to etiology and to differential diagnosis. Moreover, medical diagnosis sets out to establish not only the vital or functional prognosis of the illness, but also the most appropriate treatment. To this end, the physician has at his disposal a complex system of investigation. He first undertakes an anamnestic inquiry in order to gather the patient's recollections pertaining to the illness, and then he proceeds to direct examination using technical, instrumental, and biological means.

In the field of clinical psychoanalysis, the structure of the subject makes this way of arriving at a diagnosis impossible. The only investigational technique that the analyst has at his disposal is his listening. Because direct examination is out of the question, the only clinical material provided by the patient consists of his or her words, and so from the outset the field of clinical investigation is confined to the *act of saying* and to *what is said*.

Yet, as we know only too well, this realm of speech is saturated with lies and contaminated with imaginary constructions; it is, in fact, the very place in which fantasies unfold. It is also the place in which the subject reveals his own blindness; he does not know what he is really saying, through the words he utters, about the truth of his desire and hence about what underlies the symptom that is his desire in disguise. For this reason, a diagnosis cannot be made on the basis of objectively verifiable empirical data. Evaluation is essentially subjective, in that it depends only on the patient's discourse and is supported by the analyst's listening.

Yet even though this constitutes a radical difference with regard to medical diagnosis, there are stable guidelines within the intersubjective field. This is not a field of purely empathic interactions or of suggestive influences; psychoanalysis assumed its specific nature as a discipline as soon as Freud realized that he had to keep his interventions free of suggestion. We have every reason to believe that a topography of psychopathological complaints can indeed be mapped out, a topography, based on a method of establishing landmarks, that takes into account the most fundamental properties of its object, namely psychic causality and, in particular, the unpredictability of the workings of the unconscious.

The logical relationship between diagnosis and choice of treatment is a unique one. Although it is not a matter of logical implication as is the case in clinical medicine, the analyst must be able to rely on certain stable elements in formulating a diagnosis and in choosing the mode of treatment that that diagnosis entails. As we shall see, establishing landmarks in this way calls for great vigilance if it is not to become the kind of wild analysis that Freud condemns.

In his brief study of wild analysis, Freud (1910) offers a brilliant illustration of the care that must be taken in diagnosis and notes the dangers attendant upon interventions based on the kind of logical causality at work in the medical field. He shows us, among other things, how "wild" interpretation always stems from an overhasty causalistic reasoning grounded in a hypothetico-deductive approach that does not take into account the distance separating the act of utterance from what is being said. But an interpretation to be made to the patient does not emerge as a pure and simple logical consequence of a given diagnosis. If it did, we would be able to consult treatises on psychoanalytic therapy, just as the various medical disciplines make use of such works in their respective fields.

The sagacity Freud revealed so early in the history of psychoanalysis allows us to draw some preliminary conclusions about this problem of diagnosis. First, diagnosis is provisional; in clinical practice the act of diagnosing is, from the start, deliberately kept suspended, consigned to the future. It is all but impossible to make a reliable diagnostic evaluation before the analysis has progressed to a certain point. Yet we must nevertheless formulate a diagnostic position in order to decide the orientation of the treatment in the first place.

The provisional status of diagnosis gives rise to the second conclusion: because we are dealing with an evaluation that can be confirmed only in the course of time, this potentiality suspends, at least for awhile, the need to make an intervention that has a direct therapeutic value. The third conclusion, which follows from the first two, involves taking the time required for observation before making any decision or plan concerning the treatment. This is the time devoted to what we call the preliminary interviews, or, as Freud (1913a) puts it, the trial period. But even though this initial period is a time of observation, Freud specifies that it remains within the analytical framework:

> This preliminary experiment . . . is itself the beginning of a psychoanalysis and must conform to its rules. There may perhaps be this distinction made, that in it one lets the patient do nearly all the talking and explains nothing more

than what is absolutely necessary to get him to go on with what he is saying. [p. 124]

Freud thus emphasizes that the patient must be allowed to speak freely from the outset. Here, in fact, is the fundamental point underlying the issue of diagnosis, since diagnosis is to be defined in terms of the patient's act of speaking rather than in terms of the content of his utterances. This calls for an urgent mobilization of the analyst's ability to listen, for listening is the sole instrument of diagnostic assessment and must take priority over nosographic knowledge and causalistic reasoning.

Maud Mannoni (1965) has devoted an excellent little study to this topic, in which she stresses the immediate mobilization of listening: "This is why the first interview with the psychoanalyst is more revealing in the way speech is distorted than in what it actually contains" (p. 164). Mannoni's overall account of the developments in the initial interviews is highly relevant to the ambiguous but inescapable problem of psychoanalytic diagnosis that Freud warned us about from the very beginning.

2

Symptoms, Diagnosis, and Structural Traits

In medical practice we ordinarily try to establish correlations between specific symptoms and a given diagnosis. Indeed, therapeutic success depends to a great extent on the existence of such correlations. But if this causalistic system works, it is because the functioning of the body is itself regulated by the same mechanism; a kind of organic determinism does exist. As our knowledge of this determinism expands, the number of correlations between causes and effects increases and as a result the process of diagnosis becomes more refined.

While this principle is commonly accepted in the various medical specialties, it in no way applies to clinical psychoanalysis. The difference can be explained by the particular determinism that operates on the level of psychic processes, that is, by psychic causality, which proceeds along other pathways. The success of medical treatment is largely dependent on the regularity, the fixity, of causal events occurring in the body. But when it comes to psychic causality, while here too there is determinism, it does not follow the same patterns. In other words, there is no stable correlation between the nature of the causes and that of the effects. In the scientific domain a prediction is admissible only because it is based on a law, and a law is nothing but an objective and generalizable account of a stable connection between cause and effect. Psychic causality is not governed by laws, at least not in the strict empirical sense of the term as it is used in the exact sciences. This amounts to saying that psychoanalysis is not an exact science (Dor 1988), because the absence of lawful connection between causes and effects makes reliable prediction impossible.

So right from the beginning we must recognize that we are dealing with a situation in which we cannot make stable inferences from psychic causes to symptomatic effects in the determination of a diagnosis. Such a realization is all the more essential because it runs contrary to our usual reasoning processes. We spontaneously think in an order of Cartesian rationality that leads us to structure our explanations along systematic causal lines in the manner of scientific discourse. Challenging this order of thought based on logical implication thus requires a special effort as we begin our psychoanalytic work.

This does not mean that the connections we make are not bound by their own rigorous constraints. It is not the case that anything is possible at anyone's whim, under the pretext that we must free ourselves of our customary logical rationality. There remains a guiding thread to be followed: the utterance of the person we are listening to. It is in speech that something of the structure of the subject can be discerned. And only by relying on structure can we establish a diagnosis.

The correlations between a symptom and a given diagnosis presuppose the mobilization of a chain of intrapsychic and intersubjective processes controlled by the dynamics of the unconscious. These dynamics never unfold in the form of a logical, immediate correlation between the nature of a symptom and the particular psychic structure of the subject who manifests this symptom; what we now know about these unconscious processes makes such an immediate causal inference impossible. We have only to look at any aspect whatsoever of the unconscious process to realize that there is nothing to be gained from a deterministic approach.

A few basic examples will support this point. If we recall Freud's theory of the primary process, we enter, with him, into the very heart of the disconcerting logic of unconscious processes. To cite only one aspect, let us turn for a moment to that "instinctual vicissitude" that he calls "the turning round of an instinct upon the subject's own self":

> The turning round of an instinct upon the subject's own self is made plausible by the reflection that masochism is actually sadism turned round upon the subject's own ego, and that exhibitionism includes looking at his own body. Analytic observation, indeed, leaves us no doubt that the masochist shares in the enjoyment of the assault upon himself, and that the exhibitionist shares in the enjoyment of [the sight of] his exposure. [Freud 1915, p. 127]

Obviously, the implications of a process of this kind invalidate the notion of a direct causal relation between a symptom and a diagnosis; symptomatic sadistic activity presupposes the contradictory logic of turning against the self. Let us look further at the consequences of this observation and assume that this contradictory logic is stable with regard to unconscious processes. Thus we may posit fixed equivalents:

masochism/sadism
exhibitionism/voyeurism

But despite the stability of these equivalents, we are not justified in making an assured diagnosis on the basis of symptomatic manifestations. And in fact our everyday clinical experience belies such assurance. Let us suppose that the symptom of voyeurism logically implies exhibitionism, granting that turning against the self is a fixed law. Can we go on to infer a diagnosis of perversion on the basis of observing a symptom such as exhibitionism? By no means. Clinical experience teaches us that the exhibitionistic component can be quite salient in hysteria, as we see in hysterics' spectacular tendency to "show off."

Let us look at another example, the symptomatic activity of orderliness and tidying up, which in certain subjects can be a real hindrance when it comes to taking action. Now traditional Freudian theory has familiarized us with the idea that this behavioral peculiarity stems from an anal erotic component that is a constitutive tendency of obsessional neurosis (Freud 1908, 1913b, 1917a). When presented with this type of symptom, should we accordingly formulate a diagnosis of obsessionality? Here once again we must be very careful. Clinical experience repeatedly reveals the active presence of this symptom in certain cases of hysteria. In some hysterical women the symptom is in fact especially full blown in the attention paid to household tasks. We easily recognize it as "borrowed from the marriage"; in her wish to anticipate the other's desire, a woman can, indeed, very easily borrow this symptom from her obsessional male partner through a process of hysterical identification.

This example shows once again that there is no direct continuity between the charting of symptoms and a diagnostic classification. The gap between observation of the symptom and diagnostic assessment makes it necessary to refocus the problem in the light of the specificity of unconscious processes, and these cannot be observed directly without the patient's active participation, a participation through speech.

Here we encounter one of the most basic Freudian maxims, one that appears at the very threshold of the analytic edifice, namely that the dream is the royal road to the unconscious. But this maxim holds true only to the extent that a subject can be induced to *speak* about his or her dream. It is *discourse* that is the royal road. Without it, there would be no way to decode the workings of the unconscious. This is what Lacan (1957) had in mind in the guiding remarks made in the context of his famous "return to Freud":

> And how could a psychoanalyst of today not realize that speech is the key to that truth, when his whole experience must find in speech its instrument, its context, its material, and even the background noise of its uncertainties. . . . [W]hat the psychoanalytic experience discovers in the unconscious is the whole structure of language. [p. 147]

And as early as 1956 Lacan had emphasized the importance of speech in the experience of the unconscious:

> In order to know what goes on in analysis, we must know where speech comes from. In order to know what resistance is, we have to know what constitutes a barrier to the emergence of speech. . . . [W]hy evade the questions to which the unconscious gives rise?
>
> If so-called free association gives us access to it, does this occur through a release like those of neurological reflexes?
>
> If the drives we discover there are on the diencephalic level, or even from the rhinencephalon, how can we conceive of them as structured in terms of language?
>
> For if, from the outset, it is in language that their effects have become known, their ruses that we have since learned to recognize nonetheless denote, in their triviality as well as in their subtleties, a linguistic procedure. [pp. 461, 466]

To return more directly to the problematics of the symptom, let us call to mind Lacan's (1953) formula from the "Rome Discourse": "[T]he symptom resolves itself entirely into an analysis of language, because the symptom is itself structured like a language, because it is from language that speech must be delivered" (p. 59, translation modified). Insofar as symptom formation depends on speech and language, diagnosis must necessarily take them into account, for *structural diagnostic landmarks* occur in this register alone. Yet such structural landmarks are reliable elements in diagnostic evaluation only on condition that we can keep them separate from specific symptoms. The identity of a symptom is never anything but an artifact to be attributed to the effects of the unconscious. Diagnostic investigation requires us to find our support on this side of the symptom, in the intersubjective space that Freud (1912) described in his famous telephone metaphor as the communication of unconscious to unconscious.

This intersubjective space, in other words, is ordered by the articulation of speech. Therefore it is in the unfolding of the utterance that structural diagnostic landmarks make their appearance as breakthroughs signifying the desire of the one who is speaking. These landmarks are merely clues that signal the functioning of the subjective structure. As such, they can provide information about this functioning only because they represent signposts set up by the dynamics of desire. For in fact the specificity of a subject's structure is characterized first and foremost by a predetermined profile of the economy of his desire, which follows a stereotyped trajectory. Such stable trajectories are what I call *structural traits*. Structural diagnostic landmarks, then, appear as indices coded by structural traits that are themselves evidence of the economy of desire. Hence the necessity, if we are to be clear about the operative nature of diagnosis in psychoanalysis, of emphasizing the distinction between symptoms and structural traits. Any clinical case will illustrate the difference. (I have provided elsewhere an extensive and detailed illustration from my own treatment of a case of hysteria [Dor 1987].) Recall Freud's insistence on the fact that the symptom is always overdetermined, in that it is directly linked to the action of the primary process, especially to condensation. As a result, it presents itself as signifying material that says a lot more than may at first appear. This is a good opportunity to confirm Lacan's argument that a symptom is a metaphor, that is, a signifying substitution (Dor 1985/1996).[1]

Under these circumstances, we can understand how the nature of the symptom has only a signifying value that is as random as it is unpredictable. Being a formation of the unconscious, the symptom is, as it were, constituted by successive signifying stratifications. Yet in this stratification the choice of signifiers does not obey any fixed principle; the selection is made through the simultaneous operation of metaphoric and metonymic processes (Dor 1985/1996).[2] The signifying components that con-

---

1. Editor's note: For Lacan, a metaphor is a signifier that stands for another signifier. A symptom, therefore, represents a signifying substitution that needs to be deciphered through the chain of associations that will lead to other signifiers in the patient's discourse. Thus the symptom does not have a fixed meaning but is the effect of the processes of condensation and displacement that Freud (1900) described in *The Interpretation of Dreams.*

2. Editor's note: The metaphoric process corresponds to what Freud calls condensation, the metonymic process to Freud's displacement. Because, according to Lacan, the unconscious is structured like a language, there is an analogy between the synchronic and diachronic axes that structure language and the processes of condensation and displacement as described by Freud. In other words, the principles that regulate the structure of language are not dissimilar to the ones that organize the unconscious. Thus, for Lacan, conscious discourse and the formations of the unconscious as they appear in symptoms, slips of the tongue, dreams, or jokes are organized according to rules like the ones operative in language.

stitute the symptom thus remain directly dependent on the fantasies of the unconscious. Nevertheless, alongside the relative randomness of the choice of the signifiers involved in this unconscious formation, there is a determinacy that is inevitable, a determinacy in which the management of the signifying material takes place out of the subject's awareness. This management is characteristic of the functioning of the structure, that is, of the particular way in which desire is handled.[3] The diagnostic evaluation must therefore be devoted to identifying this mode of handling desire, which is solely responsible for bringing into play observable and stable traits.

Hence the problem of diagnosis seems to depend on a new issue: What is the constancy—if it exists—of these structural traits that in turn presuppose a certain stability in the organization of psychic structure?

---

3. Editor's note: The analyst will be led toward the discovery of this operational mode of the patient's desire because of the position that he occupies in the psychoanalytic situation. The demand for analysis implies that the patient endows the analyst with a supposed knowledge about the causes of his or her pain. Therefore the patient's discourse will disclose the nature of his or her desire through the words, distortions, or slips of the tongue that will appear in the description of what brought the patient into treatment. The analyst, as "the subject who is presumed to know," occupies a position that permits the transference to be mobilized from the very beginning of treatment.

3

The Paternal Function and Psychic Structures

It is on the basis of oedipal passions that each individual establishes a psychic structure, or what Freud called the "choice" of one's own neurosis. These oedipal love affairs are nothing but the noisy expression of the subject's relationship to the phallic function,[1] also called the paternal function. While this relationship brings order—in the sense of organizing the psychic structure—it also brings disorder, since psychic structure has the distinctive characteristic of being determined once and for all. How can an agent of order be directly linked to an agent of disorder? How are we to understand that psychic structure represents a crucial stage in the psychic economy, while at the same

---

1. Editor's note: The phallic function refers to the Freudian concept of the phallus. In Lacanian theory, the phallic function is the organizing principle of the dynamic of the subject's desire. If, in the individual's fantasy world, the phallus acts as an imaginary object that the subject will first want to incarnate and then move on to have (or to seek in a romantic partner), within the symbolic order—that is, in the unconscious realm—the phallus operates as the signifier of a loss, the symbol of the lack of complementarity between the sexes.

time this economy can prove to be the principal cause of psychopathological disorders?[2]

In trying to answer these questions, I want to focus on how the economy of desire, under the influence of the phallic function, can give rise to different types of structure. Distinguishing among these types is essential if we want to gain accurate knowledge about clinical diagnosis. Here memories of oedipal passions are all-important, for it is through their vicissitudes that the subject negotiates his or her relation to the phallus, that is, to the conjunction of desire and lack.[3]

This, of course, involves a detailed review of the entire oedipal dynamic, which is played out in the dialectic of *being* the phallus or *having* it. This is the phase in which the child moves from a position in which he or she identifies with the mother's

---

2. Elsewhere (Dor 1987) I have approached this issue by suggesting a metaphorical analogy to the self-preservation of structures as described in molecular biology.

3. Editor's note: The concept of lack, *manque à être*, refers to Lacan's theory of symbolic castration. For Freud, the resolution of the Oedipus complex is dependent on the boy's fear of castration and the girl's penis envy, whereas for Lacan both sexes must undergo the same painful but necessary process that symbolic castration entails. Lacan connects the child's submission to the prohibition of incest with his or her entrance into the structure of language. The human being's capacity to symbolize is dependent on his or her acceptance of a loss, the loss of an imaginary complementarity with the mother. As Hegel (1807/1985) pointed out, the word is the murder of the thing. This loss consists in giving up one's privileged position as the mother's phallus in order to position oneself in the social world as someone who "has the phallus" or "does not have it." Meeting this almost impossible challenge, which Lacan calls symbolic castration, will offer the individual the bittersweet guarantee that his or her desire will never die off, because it will always remain dependent on the desire of the other. The hope of finding the phallus—in the imaginary—that will guarantee the complementarity between the sexes will always be postponed, since the phallic signifier, as it is operative in the unconscious, causes desire precisely because it is the signifier of lack.

phallus to another position in which he or she renounces this identification and thus accepts symbolic castration. The child now tends to identify either with the subject who is not presumed to have the phallus or with the one who is presumed to have it. This takes place in the course of the process of symbolization that Lacan calls the metaphor of the Name of the Father.[4]

I have described this oedipal dialectic at greater length in my *Introduction to the Reading of Lacan* (Dor 1985/1997). What I want to do here is focus on certain key phases of the oedipal dynamic, those decisive moments for the subject when the stakes of the desire mobilized by the relation to the phallus are such that structural organization is most likely to occur. The various psychic structures—perverse, obsessional, hysterical, and psychotic—are determined by one or the other of these crucial phases. They are established when the reciprocal desires of the mother, the father, and the child come into conflict with regard

---

4. Editor's note: The Name of the Father (*le nom du père*) or Paternal Metaphor can be heard as both the no/*non* of the father and his name/*nom*. This pun contains the two dimensions of what Lacan understands to be symbolic castration: the negative side that enforces the prohibition of incest ("No," says the father, "you cannot be your mother's phallus, the exclusive object of her desire") and the positive side, the child's inscription in the generational order (as the son or daughter of a father and a mother), which locates the child in the social world, the realm of language. Lacan's expression "paternal metaphor" not only refers to the double meaning of the *non/nom* but also points toward language *per se* as a metaphor for what has been irreversibly lost when the child becomes a speaking subject. In speaking, the subject does not know that he or she is symbolizing, through language, the object of his or her primordial yearning. For Lacan, then, castration is not merely the fear of losing or missing the penis. It is a symbolic operation that cuts the imaginary bond between mother and child and grants the boy or the girl the ability to symbolize this loss through words. Therefore the fear of losing the penis or the frustration at not having it is grounded not in our "anatomical destiny" but in the dynamics at work within the intersubjective realm in which mother, father, and child are inscribed.

to the phallic object. As I have already emphasized a number of times, this psychic structuring is definitive. But as we move ahead with this thorny issue, I want to make it clear that, while the structure is irreversibly determined, it is also true that its functioning is susceptible to "changes in administration."

We must realize, quite simply, that as subjects we are never anything more than the effects of the signifier. It is at the direction of these signifying effects that the structure operates, and we have no control over them. The most we can do is to entertain the imaginary notion that we have some say in this management, and this is why each of us is compelled to stick to the structure of such a fantasy. But in having our say we don't change matters at all, since we give the lie to our words even as we utter them. Recall Freud's famous observation that the ego is not master in its own house. We have to recognize the inescapable implications of this statement; no one is obliged to subscribe to it, but the fact remains that this discovery of Freud's reveals a truth about the structure of the desire of the speaker. Even if, as Lacan so often repeated, we can only half-say (*mi-dire*) this truth, it is there, nonetheless, as a reminder of the nature of the structure and of the desire that attempts to express itself through that structure. To emphasize still further the irreducibility of linguistic structure, we should recall that it is all the more decisive because the choice of this structure, for a subject, is precisely the means by which he enters into the symbolic order.[5]

---

[5]Editor's note: The symbolic order is the order of language and culture, the synchronic structure in which the child is inscribed, unknowingly, through the workings of the prohibition of incest (paternal metaphor). This concept of the symbolic was first proposed by the structural anthropologist Lévi-Strauss, who demonstrated how the permutations at work in the elementary structures of kinship not only establish the prohibition of incest as the law

Accession to the symbolic, let me remind you, is accession to subjecthood as such. The psychic structure of the subject will be determined by the way he or she conquers a place in the symbolic order.

This structural organization, formed in the hidden recesses of the oedipal dialectic, is imprinted by the two powerful phases

---

that transforms nature into culture, but also reveal that language and culture are both shaped by a symbolic system operating on an unconscious level.

Lacan applied some of Lévi-Strauss's findings to the psychoanalytic field and went on to demonstrate how the child's submission to the prohibition of incest is concomitant with his or her entrance into language. He called upon the findings of structural linguistics in order to explain the complex relation between oedipal dynamics and language, using Freud's (1920) famous example of the *fort/da* game and Roman Jakobson's (1956/1971) phonology to illustrate the way in which the acquisition of language goes hand in hand with the process of primal repression. Jakobson showed that every language can be structurally reduced to twelve pairs of distinct vocal, physiological contrasts that he called bipolar phonematic oppositions. An example would be the opposition o/a in German. Therefore, when Freud's grandson was able to say *fort/da* to symbolize his mother's leaving and returning, he had at that point already assimilated unknowingly the "differential features" characteristic of the German language. In expressing joyfully, through words, his ability to control a loss, the child in this paradigmatic anecdote at the same time repressed the cause of his sadness, and his unconscious came into being. From this moment on in development, the unconscious becomes the repository of all the phonematic traces related to subsequent experiences of loss or lack.

Moreover, Lacan reinterpreted Saussure's (1916) distinctions between language/speech and signifier/signified in order to show how the structure of the unconscious and the structure of language have similar modes of operation. For Saussure, speech is determined by a system of values (language) that operates beyond the individual's control. The relation between a concept and its acoustic image does not result from a particular affinity between a word and its referent but is determined by the other signs that compose a given language. In that sense, the arbitrary relation between signifier and signified shows that language is an entity with its own laws and regulations that operate independently of the realm of existence that it represents. For Lacan, the dividing line between the signifier and the signified expresses the problem-

represented by the dimension of *being* and the dimension of *having* with regard to the phallus. In the dynamic of the passage from being to having, there are certain crucial stakes affecting the inscription of the child in the phallic function. As the regulator of the Oedipus complex, the phallic function presupposes four protagonists: the mother, the father, the child, and the phallus. This last term is the central element around which gravitate the desires of the other three. It is in this sense that Lacan used to say, in a word to the wise, that in order to do psychoanalysis one has to be able to count at least up to three. But the fact remains that, in this minimal numerical literacy, knowing how to count to three has the special meaning of knowing how to count to three starting after one, which implies counting to four. For in fact, since the phallus is element one, it is the sole reference point that enables the subject to regulate his desire in relation to the desire of an other.

As this reference point, then, the phallus is simultaneously the element that is inscribed outside the series of desires, since it is in relation to the phallus that a series of desires can be constituted, and also the element that governs the possibility of such a series, since in its absence desire cannot get free of its initial mooring. And it is from this mooring point that we have to set out if we want to be precise in specifying the crucial phases I noted above. What is most important is to define those moments in

---

atic relation between what is said consciously and what is barred from conscious discourse:

> We can say that it is in the chain of the signifiers that the meaning "insists" but that none of its elements "consists" in the signification of which it is at the moment capable.
>
> We are forced, then, to accept the notion of an incessant sliding of the signified under the signifier. [Lacan 1977, pp. 153– 154]

which the economy of the child's desire overlaps with the phallic function and comes to terms with it on the level of an inscription.

This phallic function is primarily characterized by the influence that the phallic signifier will assume for the child in the course of his oedipal development. From the structural standpoint, the first critical phase is the calling into question of the child's phallic identification, which is a primary identificatory experience in which the child is radically identified with the one and only object of the mother's desire, that is, with the object of the desire of the Other, and hence with her phallus.

Such a questioning is essential for the child, because through it he will finally encounter the "paternal figure." The paternal figure is the father not as presence but as mediator of desire. For what happens is that the intrusion of this figure of the father will introduce a new mode of vectorization into the economy of the child's desire, and this is what we mean by the paternal function. It is nothing other than the phallic function with all of the symbolic resonance that this entails.

The phallic function operates only insofar as it orients the child's desire in relation to a mediating symbolic agency, the symbolic father. In other words, we must bear in mind Lacan's fundamental distinction among the real father, the imaginary father, and the symbolic father. Elsewhere I attempt to show what a crucial difference this distinction makes in the organization of the subject's structure (Dor 1989). This is not a mere duplication of the trilogy Real, Imaginary, and Symbolic.[6]

---

6. Editor's note: Lacanian psychoanalysis reads Freud in a way that breaks down the classical dichotomies between nature and culture, individual and society, and inner and outer reality. The Real, the Imaginary, and the Symbolic decompose the psyche into three categories instead of two.

The Real is reality in its unmediated form. It is what disrupts the subject's received notions about himself and the world around him. Thus it character-

The real father is the father in the actuality of his being, that is, the father in the here and now, whether or not he is the biological father. Yet in the here and now of his history, this real father is never the one who intervenes in the course of the oedipal experience. The one who intervenes is the imaginary father, in the full meaning Freud gave to the term *imago*. The father is perceived and grasped by the child only in the form of the paternal imago, which is the father figure as it is in the child's interest to perceive him in the economy of his desire. It is also the figure of the father that the child represents to himself in accordance with the way the mother speaks to the child about him. Although there is a clear distinction between the real father and the imaginary father, the nature of the symbolic father is even more clearly demarcated, since his structuring intervention in the oedipal dialectic is as a purely signifying effect, and this signifying effect is basically what the paternal function is all about. But insofar as the paternal function is structuring, it must intervene in the register of castration (Dor 1989).

In other words, when we approach the question of the father's role in the Oedipus complex, we must be careful about

---

istically appears to the subject as a shattering enigma, because in order to make sense of it he or she will have to symbolize it, that is, to find signifiers that can ensure its control. The Imaginary is the realm of subjective experience *per se*, the world as it appears to the subject. Lacan explains the genesis of the Imaginary in the Mirror Stage, the archaic experience in which the child encounters his or her reflection in the gaze of the (m)other. From that moment on, both the child's perception of the world and his fantasies will be informed by the experience of such a gaze. The Symbolic order is the order of language and culture. It is a constraining structure imposed on the child through the Law of the Name of the Father. The repression that this law entails causes the formation of the unconscious. The Real, the Imaginary, and the Symbolic together weave the subject's reality at all times. These categories are always intertwined and are never processed by the subject in their pure or isolated form. Only a psychotic outbreak can undo the knotting of the triad.

the meaning we give to this paternal entity. We must know how the child's economy of desire is positioned according to whether it is engaged with the imaginary father or the symbolic one. At a minimum, this distinction presupposes that we be able to locate the oedipal stakes outside of reality, since the Oedipus complex is and always remains an imaginary mobilization on the child's part. It is, above all, the imaginary trajectory or route that the child constructs for himself in order to resolve subjectively the enigma posed by sexual difference.

This fact has an important clinical consequence: the real father plays an entirely secondary role in the stakes of oedipal desire. We can therefore clear up all the ambiguities that are involved in expressions such as "the presence of the father" or "the father's deficiencies." When these attributes are ascribed to the real father, they have no significant or operative bearing on the fundamentally structuring function of the symbolic father. In fact, it makes no major difference to what is at issue in the oedipal situation whether the real father is present or not, deficient or not. On the other hand, if the paternal presence or deficiency has to do with the imaginary father or the symbolic father, these attributes become decisive.

In other words, a perfect structuring psychic development can take place for the child without the presence of a real father (Dor 1989). But such a scenario presupposes the constitutive presence of the imaginary and symbolic fathers. This is no paradox. On the contrary, what is required is words, speech; the father must always be signified to the child, even if the child is not confronted with his actual presence. What is structuring for the child is being able to fantasize a father, that is, to elaborate the figure of an imaginary father on the basis of whom he will later invest a symbolic father. Should the real father be absent or "declared nonexistent," it remains the case that the structuring function is always potentially operative to the extent that the reference to an "other" is signified, in the mother's discourse, as a third agency mediating her desire, the desire of the other.

It is essentially through the imaginary father, therefore, that the oedipal child encounters the father as a disruptive element who is liable to challenge the certainty of his phallic identification. Such a challenge is never mounted in point of fact. It can intervene only because it is already there, implicitly present, in the mother's discourse. Even if the child does not take note of it immediately, he can still sense that the mother is signifying herself to him as a potential object of the father's desire. Moreover, it is this premonition that leads the child to overinterpret his own status as far as his mother is concerned. When he begins to suspect that he is not the sole object of his mother's desire, he imaginarily turns this observation into an issue of rivalry. He tries to obscure the fact that his mother can desire his father, and, at the same time, he invests the father as a rival object of his mother's desire. The father thus becomes the child's rival phallic object with regard to the mother. The challenge to the child's phallic identification can be understood only in the context of the phallic rivalry strictly speaking: "to be or not to be" the phallus, as Lacan (1957–1958) put it.

It is easy to understand why signifiers are so important in this decisive phase, since it is through discourse that the child finds the landmarks that enable him to orient his desire in such a way that it can expand toward a new horizon. But this path can also be obstructed if there are no consistent signifiers to promote the child's desire-laden inquiry into the nature of sexual difference.

Signifiers function here as a dynamic process—one could even say, as a catalyst. To the extent that the mother's discourse leaves the child in suspense on the question of the object of her desire, this question surges up even more strongly and leads him to further inquiry. This "signifying suspension" in the face of the enigma of sexual difference is fundamental, in that it forces the child to interrogate his mother's desire beyond the place where his phallic identification ends. The mother's discourse thus provides firm support for the further investigations that will lead him to the threshold of the even more enigmatic issue of castration. In other words, the mother's signifiers prove to be the decisive factor in getting the child moving toward a space other than the one in which he negotiates his immediate desires with her.

But if this impetus on the part of the child encounters even the smallest obstacle, his desiring dynamic will lapse into a state in which entropy prevails over the psychic effort he must make in order to combat it. This enforced suspension of the challenge to phallic identification can result in an encystment of the entire economy of desire, which in turn will contribute to the establishment of an irreversible psychic fixation. This is what is at issue in the organization of perverse structure, and it is precisely here that we find the origin of all the traits on which we base our diagnoses in the field of clinical psychoanalysis.

Part II

The Perverse Structure

4

The Freudian View of Perversions

Freud examined various aspects of the perverse process at different times in the course of his work. In "Three Essays on the Theory of Sexuality" (1905a) he distinguished the inversions from the perversions strictly speaking. This difference is based on the plasticity of the drive mechanism and its susceptibility to deviations with regard to the aims and objects of the drives. The inversions reflect deviations concerning the object of the drive, the perversions concerning its aim. However, going beyond this distinction, one that, with the exception of the notion of the drives, he took from the classical psychopathology of his time (Krafft-Ebing 1899), Freud emphasized the role of the perverse process in normal sexual development, describing the polymorphous perversity of infantile sexuality and its reemergence in the libidinal economy of the adult.

His argument in the "Three Essays" leads to an initial demarcation between the neuroses and the perversions that is summed up in the famous, if problematic, statement that neuroses are the negative of perversions. This formulation highlights an essential feature of the drive mechanism. Neurotic symptoms always stem from repression of the drive components of sexuality, and so Freud posits that the symptomatic nature of neurosis "[gives] expression (by conversion) to instincts which would be described as perverse in the widest sense of the word if they could be expressed directly in phantasy and action without being diverted from consciousness" (p. 165). The distinction Freud is making here between neurosis and perversion is important because, as we shall see, it presupposes that these structures are anchored differently in the oedipal dialectic.

In "Instincts and their Vicissitudes" (1915) Freud elaborates his theoretical and clinical ideas on the perverse process, specifying two "vicissitudes" characteristic of this process: "the turning round of a drive into its opposite" and "the turning round of a drive upon the subject's own self." These two operations presuppose features of drives that allow for a more unified concept of the perversions. In fact, the notion of modification with regard to the aim and the object of the drive leads to a crucial metapsychological generalization, whereby the distinction between inversions and perversions becomes, if not useless, at least inconsequential. It is the entire range of drive processes characteristic of inversions and perversions that constitutes one of the essential dimensions of the perverse process. With this generalization, Freud begins to sketch out the concept of a perverse structure, going beyond what had until then been defined stereotypically in terms of certain sexual practices.

Thus Freud unerringly sets out to seek the original metapsychological mechanism of perversion, formulating notions of the disavowal of reality (with regard to castration) and of the splitting of the ego as an intrinsic part of the functioning of the psychic apparatus. And with these two concepts we come back to the oedipal dialectic.

The Oedipus complex begins with the attribution of the phallus to the mother. This phallic attribution, in turn, derives from the question of sexual difference that, right from the start, the child finds so enigmatic. The entire imaginary journey of the Oedipus complex consists in the child's attempts to find answers to this enigma:

> In the course of these researches the child arrives at the discovery that the penis is not a possession which is common to all creatures that are like himself. . . . We know how children react to their first impressions of the absence of a penis. They disavow the fact and believe that they *do* see a penis, all the same. They gloss over the contradiction between observation and preconception by telling themselves that the penis is still small and will grow bigger presently; and they then slowly come to the emotionally significant conclusion that after all the penis had at least been there before and had been taken away afterwards. The lack of a penis is regarded as a result of castration, and so now the child is faced with the task of coming to terms with castration in relation to himself. [Freud 1923, pp. 143–144]

The phallic attribution is the conception of something that should have been there and that is thus experienced as missing. For this reason, the phallic object is a strictly imaginary one. We can therefore say that, for Freud, the issue of castration was from the beginning irreducibly linked to the imaginary dimension of the phallus and not to the organ—the penis or its absence.

To review briefly the remainder of Freud's account, the child does not willingly give up the representation of the phallic mother without which he would be abruptly confronted by the reality of sexual difference. The child sees no psychic advantage in accepting this reality as such, that is, as pure difference, for to do so would be to accept the unbearable conclusion that his own phallic identification is imaginary, and that he would therefore somehow have to give up being the one and only object of his mother's desire. By directing his desire toward the other, the child mobilizes this protective fantasy that dismisses the reality of sexual difference in favor of a construction based on the imaginary elaboration of a supposedly missing object—the phallus—and on a notion of sexual difference that turns on being castrated or not being castrated. Because of this fantasmatic reasoning, Freud explains, the confrontation with castration will inevitably arouse anxiety in the child. Such an imaginary construction can only encourage the belief in the threat of castration; the child could also be castrated, since this may have happened to his mother.

It is at this point that Freud places the onset of castration anxiety and hence of the defensive reactions that are intended to neutralize it. These defensive psychic constructions are evidence not only of the child's refusal to accept sexual difference, but also of the psychic effort that he has to expend prematurely in order to escape castration. Freud shows how these defenses will in large measure predetermine and orient the course of the psychic economy according to certain modalities that we now refer to as psychic structures.

Freud distinguishes three possible ways of dealing with castration anxiety, two in which the subject accepts the occurrence of castration only on condition that it can be continually transgressed, and another in which he accepts it, whether he wants to or not, but deploys an entire range of symptoms that express nostalgia for a precastrated state. The first outcome is that of the perversions, the second that of the symptomatic nostalgia of hysterical and obsessional neurosis.

As Freud sees it, then, the perverse structure seems to originate in castration anxiety and in the mobilization of defenses

against it. He calls attention to two defensive processes characteristic of the perverse organization: fixation (and regression)
and the denial of reality. According to him, these mechanisms
are constitutive of homosexuality and fetishism, respectively.

Homosexuality is basically the result of a defensive narcissistic reaction in the face of castration, in the course of which
the child electively fixates on the representation of a woman
endowed with a penis. This representation will actively persist
in the unconscious and influence future libidinal development.
A careful reading of "On the Sexual Theories of Children"
(1908a) calls for a comment here. The organization of the perverse process in its homosexual variant implicitly refers to *male*
homosexuality; this clearly suggests that male homosexuality
derives from a perverse structure, but it remains an open question whether the same is true of female homosexuality. It is
particularly important to keep this problem in mind from the
diagnostic standpoint. In fact, the very idea that a perverse structure exists in women is quite problematical, although to be sure
we can observe perverse behaviors in women (Dor 1991). In
short, the psychic system of male homosexuality is radically
different from the one we find in the female variety.

This theory is confirmed by the other aspect of perverse
functioning mentioned earlier, namely fetishism. Clinically, fetishism appears as an exclusively male operation. The defensive
process at work here is more complex than the one we looked
at in connection with homosexuality. It essentially amounts to
the disavowal or denial of reality, the refusal to acknowledge the
reality of a traumatic perception—the absence of a penis in the
mother and in all women. The defensive strategy put in place
by denial of reality has as a correlative mechanism the elaboration of a substitute formation.

This operation unfolds in two phases. First, there is the
disavowal *per se* of reality, the maintaining of a strictly infantile

attitude in the face of women's lack of a penis. Although the subject perceives this absence, he dismisses it in order to neutralize castration anxiety. However, in contrast to what occurs in homosexuality, the fixation on the representation of the phallic mother is more labile and hence permits a compromise formation. Since a woman does not have a penis in reality, the fetishist will, in the second phase, embody the supposedly missing object in another object in reality, the fetish. The fetish becomes the incarnation of the phallus, "a substitute for the woman's (the mother's) penis that the little boy once believed in and—for reasons familiar to us—does not want to give up" (Freud 1927, pp. 152–153).

The fetish thus mediates several defensive operations. It allows the subject not to give up the phallus; it allows him to ward off castration anxiety; and, finally, it allows him to choose a woman as his sexual object in that she is presumed to possess the phallus. This solution therefore enables the fetishist to avoid the homosexual outcome.

The progressive exploration of the perverse process led Freud, via fetishism, to formulate the concept of the splitting of the ego, the intrapsychic splitting essential to the description of the subject's psychological structure. Fetishism is characterized by a unique psychic mechanism, the coexistence of two mutually exclusive psychic formations: on the one hand the acknowledgment of the absence of the penis in women, and on the other hand the disavowal of the reality of this acknowledgment. There is a total contradiction between the subject's denial of the reality of absence and the establishment of the fetish as an eloquent witness to the permanent recognition of that absence. And yet, as Freud observes, these two psychic contents, mutually exclusive with regard to reality, coexist in the psychic apparatus without ever influencing one another. He therefore posits the existence of a splitting of the ego, and we see such splitting again and again as an intrinsic element of the subject's structure as such. Freud discusses this issue in a number of works, especially in connection with the clinical treatment of psychosis (Freud 1924a,b, 1938).

5

The Anchoring Point of Perversions

Let us return to the oedipal dialectic at the point where the original phallic identification is challenged by the intrusion of an imaginary father fantasized by the child as his phallic rival for the status of being the sole object of the mother's desire. The phallic stakes here concern the father's interference in the mother's *jouissance*, her pleasure and gratification. At the same time as he discovers this competition, the child discovers two orders of reality that from now on will call into question the trajectory of his desire. In the first place, it becomes clear that he is not the sole object of the mother's desire. This new situation opens up the possibility that the child will discover that his mother has a desire that is other than the desire she has for him. In the second place, the child discovers that his mother is lacking, that she is in no way fulfilled by the child insofar as he identifies with what he believes to be the sole object of her desire, that is, with the phallus. This twofold occurrence is the field of action onto which the father enters, in a position that can only be one of rivalry.

We shall rediscover the trace of this rivalry later on, in the form of a typical structural trait of perversion, namely defiance. And defiance leads inexorably to transgression, the complementary structural trait that is inseparable from it.

What establishes and consolidates the imaginary phallic rivalry is the stealthy development of a premonition, the consequences of which will turn out to be irreversible, concerning the question of sexual difference. The child foresees a new universe of *jouissance* behind the paternal figure, a realm that seems radically alien because it seems to the child to be forbidden to him. This is a realm of *jouissance* from which he is excluded. It is through this premonition that the child senses the existence of the implacable order of castration that, in a certain way, he wants to avoid completely. At the same time, this experience can represent the beginning of new knowledge about the other's desire, and thus we can understand why the child vacillates when it comes to his phallic identification. Similarly, we can see how castration anxiety can be mobilized around this paternal incursion that confronts the child not only with a potential new orientation of his desire, but also with the attendant issues of *jouissance*.

As the oedipal situation evolves, such a stasis of desire is inevitable. And yet this is a decisive occurrence, since it is in fact here that the pervert plays out the destiny of his own structure. Although he remains captive in this stasis of desire, the child can still find there a definitive mode of inscription in the phallic function. Indeed, for him, everything hangs in this balance that may or may not tip in the direction of a new stage in the development of his economy of desire, the stage of dynamic movement toward the acceptance of castration.

The pervert never stops fighting this acceptance of castration, and he is never able to engage with it as a full participant in his economy of desire. For the dynamic movement that propels the child toward the unsymbolized Real of sexual difference depends on his or her capacity to accept the loss inherent in the dynamic of desire. It is only when the child is in a position to symbolize sexual difference that he or she will be saved from the law of "all or nothing." This hovering in the balance is what eludes the pervert, in that he prematurely traps himself in the representation of *a lack that cannot be symbolized*. Such an unsymbolizable lack is what will alienate him in a never-ending psychic protest set in motion by denial or disavowal concerning his mother's castration.

To put it differently, this is a moment at which, for the child who will develop a perverse structure, there is a blocking of access to symbolic castration, to acceptance that the reality of sexual difference is the sole cause of desire. It is obvious that the lack signified by the father's intrusion is precisely what is needed to get the child's desire moving toward a new dynamic. For, at this moment of vacillation, the issue of the signifier of lack in the other is implicitly raised.[1] I am referring here to the sensitization of the child to the dimension of the symbolic father, the psychic premonition that the child must confront if he is to renounce his representation of the imaginary father.[2] Only the mediation of this signifier of lack in the other can make the paternal figure into something other than a rival phallic object. The signifier of lack in the other is logically what will lead the child to abandon the register of *being* the phallus in favor of the register of *having* it.

---

1. Editor's note: That is, the mother cannot convey to the child the ultimate "word" that will reassure him or her about his or her status as her phallic object, and alternatively the fantasized, imaginary, all-threatening father can no longer present himself as the child's absolute rival object.

2. Editor's note: His fantasy of an all-powerful father.

The passage from being to having can occur only to the extent that the father appears to the child as having what the mother desires—or, more precisely, as being presumed to have what the mother, for her part, is presumed to desire from him. This phallic attribution is what establishes him as a symbolic father, the father as representative of the Law for the child, as structuring mediator of the prohibition of incest.

It is precisely this shadow cast by the symbolic father that the pervert will ignore from the moment the question arises for him of acknowledging something on the order of lack in the other. The aim of his disavowal, that is, his protest, is to reject any possibility of symbolization of this lack. The result is the pervert's typical mode of functioning, in which a truth concerning the mother's desire is simultaneously encountered and denied. In other words, the child locks himself into the following contradiction: the intrusion of the paternal figure leads him to suspect that the mother, who does not have the phallus, desires the father because he "is" it or "has" it; on the other hand, if the mother does not have it, maybe she can have it anyway. To bring this about, he has only to attribute the phallus to her and maintain the attribution in the imaginary register. This imaginary maintenance is what negates sexual difference and the lack that it represents. The coexistence of these two options with regard to the phallic object gives the economy of the pervert's desire its characteristic profile and structure.

This structure is organized according to a law that does not allow the subject to envision any possibility of desire once castration has been acknowledged. It is a blind law that tends to substitute itself for the Law of the Father, that is, for the only law that can orient the child's desire toward a destiny that is not blocked off from the outset. This is another way of saying that what obstructs the pervert's assumption of desire is the law underlying it: an imperative law of desire that is intent on never referring to the desire of the other. For only the Law of the Father imposes a structure on desire such that desire is fundamentally the desire of the other's desire.

Insofar as the Law of the Father is denied as the mediating law of desire, the desiring dynamics of the pervert become fixated at an archaic level. Confronted with the necessity of renouncing the primal object of his desire, the child prefers to renounce desire as such, that is, to renounce the new modality of psychic development that is required by castration. It is as if castration anxiety, motivating the child not to give up the object of his desire, immobilizes him at this point. He remains stuck in a defensive process that, very early on, makes him resistant to the psychic effort that he must generate; this is the effort that will lead to the understanding that it is precisely the renunciation of the primal object of desire that, in fact, preserves the possibility of desire by conferring a new status upon it. This new status, brought about by the paternal function, establishes a *right to desire*, in the sense of desiring the desire of the other.

Because of his particular psychic economy, the pervert is excluded from this right to desire and remains fixed in an imperative, blind pattern of action in which he ceaselessly tries to demonstrate that his law, not the law of the other, is the sole law of desire. This enables us to understand the various mechanisms of perverse functioning and the structural traits that characterize it.

I have already noted that defiance and transgression are the only two possible outcomes for perverse desire. Denial, or even disavowal, basically concerns the question of the mother's desire for the father. In this sense, it is first and foremost denial of sexual difference. As Freud correctly observed, however, such disavowal can set in only to the extent that the pervert somehow acknowledges this desire of the mother for the father. Something can be denied only if one previously knew about it. In his own way, the pervert is well aware of the reality of sexual difference. What he refuses are its implications, of which the main one is that it is this very difference that is the signifying cause of desire. Thus the pervert tries to maintain the possibility of a *jouissance* that could do without this signifying cause.

By constantly provoking the law, the pervert assures himself that it is still there and that he can encounter it. In this sense, transgression is the inevitable correlative of defiance. There is no more efficient way to assure oneself of the existence of the law than to try hard to transgress the prohibitions and rules that symbolically relate back to that law. The more he defies or even transgresses the law, the more he feels the need to make sure that such a law originates in sexual difference and refers to the prohibition of incest.

6

The Differential Diagnosis of Perversions, Hysteria, and Obsessional Neurosis

Defiance and transgression can be observed in structures other than the perverse, namely in obsessional neurosis and hysteria. In these structures, however, transgression is not linked to defiance in the same way.

OBSESSIONAL NEUROSIS

Defiance is clearly present in certain symptomatic behaviors of obsessionals. Think of their compulsion to engage in all forms of competition or of regulation of mastery; what underlies these situations is the problem of defying a real or imagined adversary.

But this active defiance is inversely proportional to any possibility of transgression. The obsessional can mount his all-out defiance only in the context of a legitimate battle; indeed, he is very concerned about the rules of combat and the least failure to observe them. We can therefore conclude that the obsessional tries desperately—albeit unconsciously—to become a pervert, but always fails in the attempt.

The more the obsessional sets himself up as the champion of legality, the more he struggles, unknowingly, against his desire to transgress. What he doesn't know—or doesn't want to know—about defiance is that he is its sole protagonist. He needs to create an imaginary situation of adversity in order to engage in defiance, for in that way he can misrecognize that it is almost always he who is throwing down gauntlets to himself. And he picks them up all the more willingly because they allow him to make a great expenditure of energy.

The transgression enacted by obsessionals corresponds to their headlong flight in the face of their own desire. It is by no means unusual, in this attempt to escape, for the desire to run faster than the obsessional who wants to remain ignorant of it. The fleeing subject is then overtaken by the enactment of this desire, which for the most part he undergoes passively. At these moments, when the subject is as it were kidnapped by his own desire, the desire is often actualized in transgression. Most of the time these are minor offenses, but because they are dramatized by the subject they may seem spectacular in a manner reminiscent of perverse transgression. Motor activity frequently fuels this dramatization, an acting out in which the obsessional permits himself to come under the influence of his desire, with all its attendant *jouissance*.

HYSTERIA

We also find defiance in the hysterical structure. What underlies transgression here is the urgent issue of identification itself that arises from the phallic logic, and the related question of sexual identity. It is because of the ambivalence of hysterics with regard to their sexual identity that hysterical desire can express itself in ways that are similar to what we find in the perverse profile.

This perverse ambivalence appears in the homosexual scenarios often acted out by hysterics. We may also recall the perverse *jouissance* of hysterics in "bringing the truth to light." Here we find the classic hysterical position that Lacan described in terms of the trenchant Hegelian concept of the "beautiful soul," the *belle âme*.[1] For in fact there is no hysteria without the disposition to bring the truth to light in an idealistic way, at one time or another, even if this involves exposing the nature of the other's desire in the presence of a third party. This is especially the case in any triangular situation where the revelation of a truth concerning the one party actually turns out to disarm or question the desire of the other party.

But then again, in hysteria, the aspect of transgression is weaker than in the perversions. And, while such a thing as hysterical defiance undoubtedly exists, this defiance is a second-rate one because it is never sustained by the fundamental challenge to the paternal law, to the phallic logic of the signifier of castration. For in hysteria the signifier of castration *is* symbolized. The price that had to be paid for this symbolization appears in the register of phallic nostalgia.[2] It is this nostalgia, moreover, that gives hysteria its pervasively spectacular and overwhelming char-

---

1. Editor's note: "[T]he *belle âme* . . . does not recognize his very own *raison d'être* in the disorder that he denounces in the world" (Lacan 1977, p. 70).

2. Editor's note: For hysterics, in other words, symbolic castration has occurred; they have accepted the other's lack. The nostalgia that they experience leads to acting out that remains staged in the imaginary. They can only pretend to defy the reality of their castration.

acter. The nostalgic scenarios represent poetic dramatizations in a fantasized state of grace. Yet, as we know, a state of grace is of psychic interest only because it is purely imaginary; as soon as it is embodied in reality the hysterical display gets the upper hand, and the hysteric, driven into the corner of his or her masquerade, escapes in a pirouette.

The hysteric is especially fond of the element of make-believe, insofar as it gives him or her a way to undertake and sustain defiance. This defiance, as such, is a strategy for claiming the phallus. As a characteristic example, consider the classic fantasy of the hysterical woman identified with a prostitute. In a formidable act of defiance, such a woman will walk up and down the street or sit in her car in a strategic place until the opportunity presents itself to say to some imprudent man who solicits her, "I'm not the kind of woman you seem to think I am!"

Another aspect of feminine hysterical defiance is readily tested out in the phallic dispute that often determines her relationship with a male partner. Here we find all those situations in which she challenges the man by saying, "Without me, you'd be nothing," which is another way of saying, "I defy you to prove to me that you really have what you're supposed to have." If the partner is rash enough to undertake such a demonstration, the hysteric presses further and further ahead in her challenge.

In the case of masculine hysteria, defiance likewise comes under the heading of phallic attribution. It is as if the subject engages in defiance only when called upon by the other's desire. In this particular dialectic of desire, the hysterical man hurls an intolerable challenge at himself, one that results from an equation of desire with virility. For him, to be desirable necessarily implies that he be able to prove his virility with regard to a woman. In this sense, the hysterical man gets caught in his own implacable challenge and cannot desire a woman except through the fantasy in which she succumbs to the demonstration of his virility. In such a system it is therefore the woman's *jouissance* that becomes the sign of her capitulation before phallic omnipotence. It is not surprising that the male hysteric gets bogged down in this intolerable challenge and has to respond to it through familiar symptomatic behavior: premature ejaculation or impotence. I shall be examining this issue in more detail in Chapter 14, in the context of the structural description of hysteria.

7

The Pervert and the Law of the Father

The problematics of denial have a distinctive organization in the pervert. Whereas in hysteria and obsessional neurosis it is the imaginary possession of the phallic object that is challenged, in the perversions the fundamental defiance is directed to the Law of the Father. It occurs within the dialectic of *being* or *not being* the phallus. For the obsessional and the hysteric, on the other hand, the defiance concerning the possession of the phallic object involves the alternatives of *having* or *not having* it. Yet this initial categorization is not precise enough to be operational clinically.

It is important to emphasize how imperative it is that the pervert apply the law of *his own* desire as the only law of desire that he recognizes. This desire of his is not based on the law of the Other's desire, which is, originally, the father's law. The father, as Lacan says, "lays down the law" for the mother and the child, but the pervert makes a continual effort to defy the Law of the Father with all that that law entails with regard to the symbolization of lack, that is, castration. When all is said and done,

what he is doing in defying the paternal law is refusing to sub-
ordinate his desire to the law of the other's desire. The pervert
thereby enacts two options: the predominance of the law of his
own desire as the only possible law of desire, and the misrecognition of the law of the other's desire as the mediator of everyone's
desire. Perverse *jouissance* is entirely constituted between these
two poles and is sustained by a strategy that is impossible, but
the point of which is to make the other party question the lim-
iting nature of the Law of the Father.

The pervert, therefore, is led to posit this law (and castration) as an existing limit so that he can then go on all the more
effectively to demonstrate that it is not a limit, in the sense that
one can always take the chance of overstepping it. For the pervert derives the full voluptuous benefit of his *jouissance* in this
strategy of transgression. Yet such a strategy requires a real or
imaginary accomplice, a witness deceived by the fantasmatic con-
juring trick in which the pervert is engrossed with respect to castration. Among the potential witnesses the mother is, if not the
original, at least the privileged one, as we shall see further on.

The following passage from Jean Clavreul (1981) illustrates
the way in which the presence of this complicit witness is indispensable to the pervert's enactments:

> It is clear that it is as bearer of a gaze that the Other will be
> the partner, and above all the accomplice, in the *perverse act*.
> This touches on the radical distinction between perverse
> practice, where the gaze of the Other is absolutely necessary
> to the complicity without which the field of illusion would
> not exist, and *perverse fantasy*, which not only manages very
> well without the Other's gaze, but depends for its success
> on self-satisfaction in the solitude of the masturbatory act.
> If the perverse act is clearly distinct from the enacted fan-
> tasy, the boundary line between them is the gaze of the Other:

this gaze provides a necessary *complicity* for the pervert, whereas it is experienced as *denunciatory* by the normal or neurotic subject.[1]

To the extent that the other is his tacit accomplice, the pervert can mobilize his defiance as a means of access to *jouissance*. But regardless of the variety of ways in which it is put into effect, the perverse strategy remains the same. It always consists in leading the other astray with regard to the landmarks and the limits that determine the other's relation to the law. As Clavreul goes on to say:

> Of primary importance for the pervert is that the Other be sufficiently engaged, inscribed, in terms of acknowledged criteria—especially criteria of respectability—so that each new experience seems like a debauchery; that is, so that the Other is drawn away from his system and achieves a *jouissance* that the pervert is in all cases confident of controlling.[2]

The way in which the pervert relates to the Law of the Father is, paradoxically, seen mainly through a particular mode of relating to the mother and, beyond her, to all women. But this is not really surprising, since the pervert's disavowal bears directly on the mother's desire for the father, the very thing that is fundamentally inadmissible. This disavowal is accompanied by fantasmatic constructions formed on the basis of infantile sexual theories about castration, particularly the theory that the absence

---

1. Translator's note: Clavreul's paper "The Perverse Couple," from which this passage and the following one are taken, may be found in Schneiderman 1980; these passages, in Schneiderman's somewhat different translation, are on pp. 226–227.

2. See Dor 1987, Chapter 14 for a very telling example of such defiance, in which an aspect of an analyst's private life was corrupted.

of his mother's penis can be explained only by the castration that the father inflicted on her. This persistent feature of infantile fantasy is at the root of the special horror of castration that we find in all perverts, a horror that is all the greater because it is based on the fantasy of an actual castration.

The problem presupposes a subtle dialectic between, on the one hand, various fantasies of the mother's (and all women's) castration, and, on the other, the nature of the mother's desire for the father. The pervert oscillates between these two constellations. Either the father is responsible for having made the mother submit to the order of his desire—for having imposed on her that unjust law of desire whereby desire must always submit to the law of the other's desire—or the mother is at fault for having desired the father's desire of her own accord. In the latter case, it is on her that the pervert projects the accusation of having been an accomplice to her own castration, since she compromised herself with the father with respect to his desire.

This twofold fantasy of castration predetermines the pervert's typical behavior toward men and women. Whether it is the unjust father subjecting the mother to the law of his desire, or the weak mother accepting that law, the fantasmatic alternatives are two sides of the same coin: both are overdetermined by the horror of castration, and both are inadmissible because they confirm lack, that is, castration.

In reaction to this "horror," the pervert counters with another fantasmatic construction in which he imagines a mother who is all-powerful when it comes to desire, a mother who is not lacking. This belief entails rendering the symbolic father ineffective as the representative of the paternal function. In other words, the father is not presumed to have what the mother desires. As a result, the pervert can continue to sustain the fantasy of being the one and only object of desire that gives *jouissance* to the mother.

8

The Phallic Mother

Let us briefly return to that crucial phase of the Oedipus complex that I described as the potential anchoring point of the perversions. The term *anchoring point* refers to the occurrence of certain determinative factors that are likely to create ambiguity around the issue of phallic identification. This ambiguity involves the conjunction of two sets of determinants that can be summed up as *the mother's erotic complicity* and *the father's silent complacency.*

The mother's erotic complicity is most often manifested in the form of seduction—that is, an actual seduction and not a fantasy of seduction entertained by the child. This maternal seduction is mainly expressed through the way in which she responds to the child's sexual overtures, responses that the child inevitably experiences as signs of acknowledgment and encouragement. In this sense, the mother's response is a true call for the child's *jouissance* in that it sustains his libidinal activity toward her.

This seductive summons, however, is encumbered by a profound ambiguity. For at the same time as the child is seduced and encouraged by what his mother gives him to touch, to see, and to hear, he is also tormented by her muteness when it comes to her desire for the father. Even if, in the shared erotic complicity of mother and child, the latter is assured that the father does not mediate his mother's desire, the father nonetheless appears as an intruder. Matters are made even worse if the mother, while she does not confirm to the child that she desires the father, also does not rule out that possibility. What she most often does is sustain a disturbing ambiguity with regard to the place of the father in her desire. The child's libidinal activity toward the mother is entirely geared to this equivocation. He tries to seduce her further and further, in the hope of removing his uncertainty about the father's intrusion.

It is here, in the domain of phallic rivalry, that we find the origin of the pervert's tendency to ridicule and defy paternal authority. Moreover, this derision is very often encouraged by the mother, implicitly through her silence or even more decisively through her direct reference. The mother may even make a lying display of the paternal agency as mediating her desire, the lie being her leading the child to see how inconsistent she herself is about this mediation. The child is therefore all the more tormented because he is a captive twice over: he is a captive of maternal seduction and of a prohibition that, to be sure, she signifies to him, but at the same time as she gives him to understand that the prohibition is inconsistent. This is the first step toward transgression.

This equivocation on the mother's part has a decisive influence on the child only because it is in some sense reinforced by the father. This reinforcement reflects the father's willingness to let himself be deprived of his symbolic function. In this silent complacency, the father delegates his word to the mother, with all the ambiguity that this implies.

We come here to a fundamental clinical issue, the differential diagnosis between the perverse structure and the organization of psychotic processes. In the case of the perversions, the signification of the law is maintained. Although the law is delegated in a problematical manner to the mother's initiative, the child is never subjected to a maternal law of desire that is not referred to the Law of the Father. As Lacan puts it, the pervert's mother is not an "outlaw" mother but a phallic one.[1] The child does indeed remain confronted with a signification of desire that refers to the Name of the Father; the problem is that this signification of desire subjected to the desire of the other is not so signified by the father. The father's complacency sustains the ambiguity by allowing the mother's discourse to be the agent of the prohibition. The child thus psychically invests an equivocation between a seductive mother who encourages the child to arouse her sexually and a threatening, forbidding mother who serves as the go-between for the father's symbolic word. The child, held captive in this intermediate world, develops the fantasy of the all-powerful mother, the phallic mother.

The imago of this phallic mother will determine the pervert's later relations with other women. He will not renounce women even though, as in the case of homosexuality, he may look for them in other men.

It is clear, then, that certain structural features that express the ambiguous relation between the pervert's desire and the other's desire are organized in opposite pairs. Thus we find the alterna-

---

1. Editor's note: According to Lacan, the best example of the "outlaw" mother is the mother of Schreber (Freud 1911), who could not recognize the Law of the Father because her husband was himself identified with "the law" (he was promulgating his own educational laws). Schreber's real father presented himself as a symbolic father and not as the representative of the law. (See Lacan 1977, pp. 179–221.)

tives mentioned above: the nonlacking mother and the castrated mother. As a rule the pervert oscillates between the fantasmatic representations of these two feminine objects, endlessly seeking their closest approximations in reality. A woman can therefore appear to him as a virgin, a saint, or else as a repulsive whore.

The woman who incarnates the phallic mother will be fantasized as totally ideal. In this idealization we find that the pervert continues to protect himself from the mother as possible object of desire. This idealized, omnipotent woman is unsullied by any desire, a pure and perfect object, forbidden and hence untouchable, out of reach. She is the very prototype of the feminine ideal from whom he can expect only benevolence and protection; consider, for example, the privileged role that certain women play for male homosexuals.

But a woman can also represent the repulsive mother, repugnant because she is sexual, that is, desirable and desirous with regard to the father. In that case this woman/mother is relegated to the role of prostitute, of a despised object offered to the desire of everyone because she is not reserved solely for the purposes of the pervert's desire. She is the woman marked by the horror of castration. We can understand why the pervert feels that he has to despise the female genital: it is castrated, fantasized as a repellent and dangerous wound from which he must distance himself if he is not to lose his own penis in succumbing to desire. Indeed, the female genital is all the more vile because it makes sexual pleasure possible, and it must therefore be mistreated and abused. The desirable and desiring woman must be avoided at all costs if one is to escape perdition—that is, essentially, loss and lack.

9

A New Differential Diagnosis between Neurotic Structures and Perversions

Although in this paradoxical relation to women we can isolate structural traits characteristic of perversion, we must once again clarify certain points of differential diagnosis with respect to neurotic structures.

OBSESSIONAL NEUROSIS

His particular problematics of desire can lead an obsessional to certain stereotypical behaviors toward women that might, at first glance, remind us of perverts' attitude toward them. Consider, for example, how certain obsessionals worship their women. This worship seems to be sustained, at least in some cases, by the same absolute idealization of the woman that we find in the perversions. The elaborate oratorical and material measures that obsessionals take in courting the women they desire can easily turn into a sort of veneration that resembles the pervert's relation to the idealized untouchable woman. By putting the woman at arm's length, however, the obsessional expresses the very dynamics of his desire. His sole purpose in introducing a distance between the desired, untouchable woman and himself is to remain unaware of his desire. The woman is not placed apart as a pure, forbidden, unattainable being without desire in order to reinforce the needed fantasy of an all-powerful phallic woman. In the case of obsessional neurosis, the subject must prevent himself from knowing that he desires her, lest he feel himself to be at risk.

Another aspect of obsessional logic likewise illustrates the way in which the woman is viewed as an idealized object. Some obsessional men tend to lock up the woman they desire in the archives, as it were, to place her under a bell jar like a precious collector's item that must be kept out of reach, reducing her to an object of possession and accidentally to an object of consumption. Here again the woman is worshipped as quasi-untouchable; the essential point is that she be eternally present. The subject can actually end up never touching her anymore. This will be discussed in more detail in Chapter 18.

In this common tendency of obsessional neurotics we find one of the archaic dimensions of the infantile despotism that gives free rein to the impulse to mastery, to control over the object. The more the woman is reduced to being an object neither desirous nor desirable, the more the obsessional, struggling with the problem of possessing the object, is reassured. And it is in this stifling of the other's desire that he succeeds best in maintaining the logic of his own desire; as a mother substitute, the woman must remain entirely fulfilled by the presence of the subject, who is thus identified with her phallus. By putting the woman on ice in this way, the obsessional manages to sustain the compromise that governs his desire. This putting on ice, moreover, is part of his need to bring order, to bring things into line.

So that his object may remain in this quasi-inanimate—that is, non-desirous—state, the obsessional is prepared to offer the woman what amounts to a cult. This worship is one of the worst attitudes to take toward a woman, since it tends to neutralize in advance any desirous inclination on her part. To achieve his goal, the subject will nourish the abiding fantasy that he can do everything for her, give her everything, so that she will lack nothing. Nothing is too expensive as long as the object does not move, does not make any claims, and thus remains without demand. The woman is thus a prisoner of this frightful logic: "A place for each thing and each thing in its place." This, in effect, is the outward manifestation of the world of objects invested with the obsessional's desire. When the dynamics of desire are virtually dead, then and only then can he silently enjoy the misfortune of his desire.

But of course things don't happen that way. Because the woman is not completely dead, sooner or later the obsessional is doomed to come up against the pain of disorder. In fact, once the adored cult object, untouchable and untouched, begins to stir, disorder is underway. As soon as the woman appears desirable in the eyes of an other, the obsessional's supposedly immutable universe becomes shaky. In these circumstances, the loved one no longer has anything to do with an idealized object. She does not, however, become an object of iniquity, of vile and loathsome repulsion as in the case of the pervert. On the contrary, the woman now becomes an object who can flee, who can be lost, who escapes control, whence the obsessional's pitiful maneuvers to gain back the lost object.

In contrast to the pervert, who avoids and mistreats his repulsive object, the obsessional cannot do too much in order to obtain forgiveness. He willingly becomes an overwhelmed, guilty martyr, ready to pay anything, endure anything, so that matters will return to the way they were. In the name of this deadly order, the obsessional can make himself more hysterical than any true hysteric if only the object will return and stay with him. The important thing is magically to cancel out the lack; the feminine object must return to her place as the inert object without desire. Yet experience shows that the best sacrifices are to no avail. The rift introduced by the sudden appearance of the other's desire inexorably leads the obsessional to the register of loss, that is, of castration. This constitutes the crucial difference that worries the obsessional, in contrast to the pervert.

For the obsessional does not have at his disposal the pervert's "spare tire"; he can find no support in the denial of castration, that imaginary representation through which the pervert manages to keep his *jouissance* going. The idealization of the woman in obsessional neurosis is merely the creation of a magical fantasy that can never be an invulnerable rampart. The first sign of the other's desire is always critical, because it forces the obsessional to call into question the secondary gains of his neurosis; it is a reminder of castration and of the other's lack. Where the pervert cherishes the illusion of the feminine ideal that he himself has crafted, the obsessional wears himself out trying to restore an ideal that, for him, is nothing more than a vestige of oedipal prehistory, a nostalgia for the phallic identification that, like it or not, he had to exchange for the discomfort of *having* imposed by the Law of the Father. In this sense, we can say that obsessionals are romantics of the state of "being."[1]

---

1. Editor's note: In Lacanian theory, "being the phallus" refers to the blissful time when the child experienced himself or herself as that which could fulfill the mother's desire: being her phallus or being at one with the phallic mother.

HYSTERIA

We can also point out several differential features between male hysteria and the perversions in connection with the relationship to women.

In male hysteria, however, the situation is more vivid and rich than in obsessional neurosis. The relationship to women, although in some respects reminiscent of the pervert's relationship to his object, is ambiguous, because the hysterical structure lends itself to perverse manifestations. The hysterical man's relationship to the female other is most often alienated, right from the start, in his representation of the woman as idealized, placed on an inaccessible pedestal. But here we are not dealing with a pure, untouchable virgin who feels no desire. On the contrary, the woman is exalted as a valuable object precisely because she is desirable and desiring. She functions for the hysteric as a means of enhancing his prestige.

The woman must be pitilessly seductive, always offered to the gaze of the fascinated and envious other, if the subject is to idealize her. What matters to him is that she never fall from that place lest she immediately lose all her seductive advantages. Should she be dethroned, she becomes a threatening, hated object who must be destroyed. She must atone for her fall from the pedestal, the pedestal on which the hysteric's libidinal economy had placed her for the sake of his own comfort.

There is, of course, quite a subtle interplay between the woman idealized as a showpiece and the woman suddenly dethroned and responsible for all ills. We find here the hysteric's ambivalent relation to the phallus (see Chapter 14). For the male hysteric, woman constitutes the object par excellence that allows him to get his bearings with regard to possession of the phallus.

As we shall see further on, the problematics of the phallus, for the hysteric, remain strictly confined to *not having it*. Because the hysterical male does not experience himself as having the phallus, he tends to respond to a woman's desire as if he did not have a penis, or did not have it completely, whence the familiar symptom picture of impotence or premature ejaculation.

This accounts for the hysteric's sudden turnabout in his representation of the woman. All is well as long as she is the seductive and brilliant object who enhances his prestige, since she serves as an object of phallic admiration offered to everyone's gaze. The hysteric can thereby consolidate his symptom, which consists of thinking that he has been deprived of the phallus— yet it is still available to him through the woman, a brightly shining object in the gaze of others. The woman is thus a jealously guarded possession even though, at the same time, she is held out for unrestricted admiration. And the more she is coveted by others, the more the hysteric receives the paradoxical confirmation that this is so only because it is *his* phallus that is being coveted through her. Thus, as long as such an object is his inalienable property, everything is for the best as far as phallic possession is concerned.

This of course presupposes that the object, for her part, will not be too desirous, or else she will find that the ideal state of affairs is becoming complicated. If the woman starts to desire, and especially if she desires her most faithful admirer, then problems arise. For what happens is that the woman's desire confronts the hysteric with the question of possession of the phallic object. If she desires, it is because she lacks something that the other is presumed to have. But this is precisely the problem! As a result, the female object becomes an almost persecutory source of concern, because she inexorably condemns the male hysteric to the test of phallic attribution. At this moment the reassurance of the woman's fascination suddenly tips over into its opposite, and this produces the whole range of symptoms that usually accompany the hysteric's sexual exchanges.

The real trouble begins when the idealized object not only reveals herself to be lacking but also starts making peremptory demands indicating desire, a desire that leads her, as it leads each of us, towards *object a*.[2] In such a pursuit the male hysteric is disqualified in advance because of his symptomatic position with regard to the phallus. It is in this dialectic that the feminine object shifts from her former idealized role to one that is all the more hateful because she now appears as an object that can be lost.

At this point the entire imaginary scenario of "ownership" is destabilized and the idealized incarnation of the phallic object disappears. We can understand why to mistreat her is, unconsciously, to destroy the mark of the lack in the feminine object, for in these moments of collapse the hysteric is confronted with the signifier of lack in the female other.[3] It seems logical that the hysteric oscillates in a stereotyped ambivalence between a hostile attitude toward the object and an expiatory one, an oscillation that expresses his permanent ambivalence toward the phallus.

But in either case the object must be mastered. This gives rise to the ostentatious hostility that the hysteric maintains toward her in order to assure himself that he possesses her. But

---

2. Editor's note: In Lacanian theory, *object a* refers to the impossible object of desire that would assure us that the complementarity between the sexes does exist and that we can find in the other that which we lack.

3. Editor's note: The signifier of lack in the female other refers not only to woman's castration in the Freudian sense, but also to the lack that is present in all of us. This lack is what makes desire for the other possible. The drama of castration consists in having to accept the lack in the (m)other and having to realize that no human being can have or be that which can fill the lack in oneself.

very soon the hysteric is overwhelmed by his own enterprise of destruction and is led to an expiatory and quasi-magical about-face in which he tries once again to enter the good graces of his love object. In this about-face we can observe the enactment of one of the most fundamental traits of the hysterical structure, the alienation of one's own desire in favor of the desire of the other. What matters is to put oneself at the service of the other in order to place her once again on the pedestal from which she had fallen. In this situation of atonement, the price of forgiveness cannot be too high and the hysteric offers himself as a victim ready to sacrifice everything for his idealized object.

The mechanisms of humiliation are sought all the more because they validate the unbearable imaginary narcissistic wound that underlies the hysteric's presentation of himself as a consummately unworthy object. We are familiar with this unworthiness: the hysteric, who finds himself unequal to his adored feminine partner, seeks the woman's absolution for the fantasmatic disaster caused by the absence of the phallic object. The unworthiness is the proof of his misfortune in not having it in the eyes of the woman who can always remedy this defect. The expiatory scenarios are endless, since the important thing is to show the infinite sacrifices the hysteric is prepared to make for the woman he loves.

In any case, what we have here is a tragic confusion between desire and love. It is as if love for the feminine object had to be offered as the exclusive pledge of desire. The more the male hysteric loves, the more he arms himself against desire. In fact, the limitless unfolding of his love serves all the better to conceal the place of the other's lack. This explains why the hysteric often presents himself as a hero sacrificed on the field of his love for the feminine other, or as a plaintive war veteran whose many sacrifices endured for the sake of his lady's honor have remained unrecognized.

To win back the lost object, the male hysteric is ready for anything. We find here the blindness that characterizes all neurosis: the greater the loving sacrifice, the more the stirrings of the other's desire are nullified. It is on the basis of this misunderstanding that the hysteric pays the price for his inscription in the phallic function and keeps his own desire unfulfilled. In other words, the hysteric's logic of desire finds its gratification in proportion to the magnitude of his expiatory debt.

One final point needs to be added concerning the link between the dismissal of the idealized feminine object and her transformation into an object of destruction. In this changeover we commonly observe a pattern that seems to occur as a kind of metapsychological gearshift and that manifests itself as an actualization of violence. What is involved here is an element of rupture that can figure forth the lack, the loss, which is the sole driving force that keeps desire alive. Behind the sensationalism of this violence (violence that is moral as well as physical), we can discern the enactment of a well-known process: the hysterical crisis. It occurs as a libidinal discharge of the erotic investment in the object of desire. Actually, we can view this fit of violence as a "hysterical crisis à la Charcot," in curtailed form but to the same effect. We have here, although on a smaller scale, the major episodes of the classic hysterical crisis. The prodromal phase is often announced by an explanatory logorrhea. The clonic phase is generally symbolized by a spectacular clastic crisis. The resolutive phase is generally characterized by typical emotional collapses, weeping, groaning, and various other lamentations. In addition, this resolutive phase always initiates the following stage, the expiatory phase of forgiveness.

It is easy to see how, in several ways, the desiring economy of the male hysteric can at first glance be mistaken for perversion. Nevertheless, this clinical picture, although it calls to mind certain perverse symptoms, has nothing in common with a perverse structure. The absolute structural difference between these two psychic organizations is determined by the hysteric's mode of inscription in the phallic function.

Part III

The Hysterical Structure

10

Hysterical Structure and Phallic Logic

Moving on to the hysterical structure, I shall try, as in the case of the perversions, to describe the fundamental structural features, to point out what, in the dialectic of desire and the problematics of the phallus, may be considered the anchoring points of hysterical organization.

There are certain key points at which the phallic logic takes a specific turn with regard to the issue of *having* the phallus or *not having* it. But although what we are dealing with in hysteria is a structural trait, it is nonetheless true that the passage from *being* to *having* is a general occurrence in the oedipal process, a universal aspect of psychic organization. What is distinctive in hysteria is the characteristic way in which the problematics of having are dealt with. As we have seen, the passage from being to having is primarily determined by the father's intervention. The imaginary father appears specifically as a depriver and a frustrator. And he also appears as a prohibitor (Dor 1989). It is because the father is acknowledged by the mother as the one who, as Lacan puts it, "lays down the law" that the child comes to realize that the mother's desire is inscribed in the dimension of *having*. Insofar as the depriving father tears the issue of the child's desire away from the dimension of *being* (being the mother's phallus), he inevitably leads the child toward the register of castration.

It is when the child begins to get some idea of castration that he discovers not only that he *is not* the phallus but also that he *does not have it*, just like the mother who, he discovers at this same time, desires it in the place where it is presumed to be found. The father thus attains his full function as symbolic father when the mother acknowledges his word as the only one that can mobilize her desire. And seeing what he experiences as this new mobilization of the mother's desire, the child establishes the imaginary father in the role of guardian of the phallus.

I want to place special emphasis on the reversal of the dialectic of being and having in the organization of hysterical structure. Lacan (1957–58) provides a valuable explanation of this point and of its impact on the castration complex:

> In order to have [the phallus] there must first have been a question of one's not having it. This possibility of castration is essential to the assumption of the fact of having the phallus. It is here that we have *the step that must be taken*, it is here that at some point, effectively, really, the father must intervene.

What is at issue in hysteria is above all the question of this "step that must be taken" in the conquest of the phallus. It is through this conquest that the child frees himself from the phallic rivalry in which he had set himself up and in which he had imaginarily placed the father. The achievement of the conquest of the phallus is precisely what Freud referred to as the waning of the

Oedipus complex. This waning, clearly, is directly dependent on the question of the father's phallic attribution, and this, in turn, is the very moment at which the logic of hysterical desire is set in motion.

As Lacan (1957–58) observes, the father must give proof of that attribution, and the hysteric's entire desiring economy is consumed by the symptomatic putting to the test of just this "giving proof." Once again Lacan explains this psychic threshold on which the hysteric stumbles neurotically:

> It is insofar as [the father] intervenes as the one who has the phallus and not as the one who is it that there can arise *that something that establishes the function of the phallus as an object desired by the mother and not only as an object of which the father can deprive her.*

The hysteric ceaselessly questions and contests the phallic attribution, oscillating around this "something" that develops out of an indeterminacy between two psychic alternatives: either the father has the phallus by right, and that is why the mother desires it in him; or the father has it only because he has taken it from the mother. It is primarily the latter option that motivates the hysteric's constant testing of the phallic attribution.

To accept that the father is the sole legitimate guardian of the phallus is to engage one's desire with regard to him on the basis of not having it. On the other hand, to contest the phallus on the grounds that the father has it only because he has deprived the mother of it is to open up the possibility of a permanent claim based on the fact that the mother, too, can have it, and in fact has the right to it.

It is easy to see how, on this level of the oedipal dialectic, every ambiguity, every ambivalence on the part of the mother and father concerning exactly where the phallic attribution is to be situated can be conducive to the organization of the hysterical process. I have suggested that obsessionals are nostalgic for the state of *being* the phallus, and we might also say that hysterics are militantly engaged in the cause of *having* it. This claim to the possession of the phallus reveals some of the most remarkable structural features of hysteria. But it should be noted that sexual difference plays a role here. The hysteric's claim will assume a gender-specific form in terms of manifest behavior, although essentially the same fantasy underlies his quest, indeed, his conquest: the subject has been unjustly deprived of the phallic attribution and must reappropriate it. Whether it is the hysterical woman "pretending she's a man," as Lacan put it, or the male hysteric tormenting himself about proving his virility, the dynamics are the same. Both entertain a fantasy prompted by the supposed possession of the phallus, which, for both, implies the admission that they do not have it.

11

Features of the Hysterical Structure

It is a commonplace in the psychoanalytic literature that the hysteric has a tendency toward conversion symptoms. Similarly, hysteria is said to be characterized by the formation of phobic symptoms, usually in connection with anxiety. While these signs are indeed of some minor diagnostic interest, they are unreliable because they are merely part of a taxonomy of symptoms. As we have seen, such clinical indications are always insufficient when it comes to a rigorous diagnostic assessment. They serve only as preliminary items of information that must be confirmed by the discovery of structural features. It is one thing to have in mind the standard clinical picture of hysteria, and quite another to make sure that such a symptomatology never serves more than a purely nosographic function.

It is generally agreed that there are three major categories of hysteria: conversion hysteria, anxiety hysteria, and traumatic hysteria. From the nosographic point of view, each of these types is distinguished from the others by specific symptoms, as set forth in one or the other psychiatric classification. But in clini-

cal psychoanalysis this system plays only a minor role. Whatever type of hysteria we are dealing with, the underlying economy
of hysterical desire remains fundamentally the same, and this
sameness can be ascertained only on the basis of structural traits,
deeper indications that point to a specific structure. One patient
may favor somatic conversion, another may manifest primarily
phobic symptoms and elements of anxiety: in both cases therapeutic intervention will be effective only if it succeeds in deac-
tivating the neurotic economy of desire, that is, if it goes beyond
symptoms to refer to the structural level.

Furthermore, we should not forget that the hysterical symptom picture is present in other structural organizations as well.
We must, therefore, pay attention to the rigorous decoding of
structural traits, as opposed to the tracking of symptoms.

Regarding these structural traits, I first want to discuss what
might be called the subjective alienation of the hysteric in his
relation to the other's desire. This is in fact one of the most
important elements that constitute the functioning of the hysterical structure. To understand its specific nature, we must go
back to the problematics of having, for this is the very epicenter
of the question of hysterical desire.

If the object of oedipal desire, the phallus, is what the hysteric basically feels he has been unjustly deprived of, he can
delegate the question of his own desire only to the one who is
supposed to have it. In this sense, he questions the dynamics of
his desire only with reference to the other, who is always presumed to possess the answer to the enigma of the origin and
workings of the desire in question.

We can see, then, how the other serves as a privileged support for identificatory processes. So-called hysterical identification (Freud 1921) originates in this alienation, and the support
can be provided by a woman as well as by a man. A hysterical

woman, for example, can easily identify with another woman if the latter is presumed to know the answer to the riddle of desire: How can one desire if one is deprived of what one is entitled to? As soon as a desirous woman presents herself as "not having it" but nevertheless desiring it in the man who is presumed to have it, such a woman appears to the hysteric as the one who can give her the answer to her question. Hence we find the hysteric coming to identify with this model.

Such an identification, of course, is never anything but a neurotic ploy, a blindness, in no way able to provide the expected response. On the contrary, it merely increases the neurotic dissatisfaction of the economy of desire. As Lacan says, it actually conceals the "step to be taken," that is, finally accepting one's lack of a phallus in order to make it possible to acquire the phallus at some future time. And indeed, accepting that one does not have the phallus means being able to identify with the woman who does not have it but who desires it in the man who is presumed to have it.

Yet the hysteric can also identify with the woman who does not have it and who, as a result, sets about to claim it. This is an identificatory strategy that I do not hesitate to call "militant identification" or "identification based on solidarity." This disposition leads to the same blindness as in the preceding instance, since it once again denies the condition that fixes the relation of the subject to the desire for the phallus.

In any case, these identificatory processes bear witness to the subjective alienation of hysterics in their relation to the desire of the other, particularly in the subordination of their desire to what they suppose, sense, even imagine ahead of time to be the desire of the other. Such an overactive imagination leaves the way open to all varieties of suggestion, and influence and suggestion always operate under two conditions. First, the other who is doing the suggesting must already have been granted a privileged position by the hysteric, and, second, the hysteric must feel that he is able to respond to what he believes the other expects from him. The privileged position is that of the Master, who is always established as such by the hysteric insofar as he is presumed to know what the hysteric is making every effort to misunderstand with regard to his desire.

In this sense, anyone can find himself, under favorable circumstances, invested with this function of mastery. The situation becomes complicated fairly often, especially when the person enthroned as Master shows no aptitude for the role. In this context Lacan very pertinently observed that the hysteric needs a master over whom he can rule. However, if the other manifests even a few of the features that the hysteric lends him in fantasy, he immediately becomes the "chosen one" in relation to whom the hysteric will proceed to develop the blindness characteristic of the impasses of his desire. All the "chosen one" has to do is confirm his fantasmatic role with a few examples of mastery in real life for the hysteric to intensify the workings of his neurotic economy.

The examination of some common scenarios can shed light on this alienation of the hysteric's desire in the other's desire. Consider, for example, the aspect of "showing someone to good advantage" that governs the intersubjective exchanges of certain couples. Hysterics have the unique tendency to set aside the expression of any personal qualities in order to highlight those of the partner. They present themselves as the unconditional defenders of the ideas, the convictions, and the choices of the other.

Generally speaking, this passion for putting oneself at the service of the other is more prevalent in feminine hysteria. Such subjects devote all their skill and talent to rejoicing in the prestige that the other derives from these talents. As for the men who lend themselves to this masquerade, they identify with the role of object shown to advantage, or status symbol, to which the hysterics have consigned them.

This self-sacrifice reveals yet another essential aspect of hysteria, namely "showing oneself." It occurs via displacement, since putting oneself at another's service always amounts to trying to display oneself through the other and to shine by reflected light. This kind of dependence always points to the renunciation of some aspect of one's own desire in favor of the other. What is taking place, therefore, is a double capture, robbing oneself in terms of the expression of one's own desire, and at the same time trapping the other by confusing oneself with him and constantly pushing to the forefront the desire one believes to be his.

This hysterical tendency assumes a number of typical forms. Thus, to please and to try to fulfill what he imagines to be the other's pleasure, the hysteric willingly undertakes a crusade of sacrificial self-abnegation; historically we find a version of this in the missionary. And let us not forget the fate of "Anna O" (Bertha Pappenheim) (Freud and Breuer 1895), who founded that famous group of benefactresses, the social workers. On the male side, think of the "war veterans" who foster the secondary gains of neurosis by boasting about all the sacrifices they made for the sake of their family, their work, or other worthwhile causes.

Although the element of *having* is a permanent substrate of the hysterical economy of desire, there are certain times at which, precisely because he does not have it, the hysteric will give preference to his identification with the phallus, that is, to *being* it. This in no way contradicts the former position. On the contrary, it is in fact an entailment of the hysterical relation to having, and in this sense it is yet another characteristic structural feature of hysteria.

In every hysteric there remain, in a more or less intrusive way, the traces of an archaic lament based on a claim of love from the mother. For the hysteric often experiences himself as not having been loved enough by the other, as not having received the full evidence of the love he expected from his mother. This frustration in love always comes under the heading of what is at stake with regard to the phallus. Thus the hysteric sees himself as a pathetic object of his mother's desire, as opposed to what would be a complete and ideal object, the phallus.

The most obvious effect of this devalued relation to the object of the mother's desire is found in the area of the hysteric's identity. This identity is always unsatisfactory, deficient—in other words, partial—in comparison with an ideal, fully realized identity; hence the efforts, as futile as they are insatiable, that the hysteric makes in order to achieve that identity. The fantasy underlying this industrious activity is, clearly, that of becoming the other's ideal object for the first time. The strength of the presupposition that one has never before been that ideal object determines the distinctive configuration of the hysterical economy of desire.

Early on, Freud called attention to the degree to which the hysteric's chief desire is *that his desire remain unsatisfied*—see the discussion of the "dream of smoked salmon" (Freud 1900, pp. 147–151). Such a subject confines himself within an irrefutable psychic logic: in order to maintain his desire, he tries never to supply a possible fulfilling object for that desire, and in this way the resulting dissatisfaction remobilizes his desire in an aspiration, always more and more remote, toward an ideal of being.

Insofar as what the hysteric is pursuing is, above all, organized around this identification with the ideal object of the other's desire, all his efforts are in the service of phallic identification. It is not surprising, therefore, to note the hysteric's intense attraction toward any situation in which this imaginary identification can be brought onstage. Hence we find what is commonly referred to as the phallic narcissism of hysterics. Since phallic narcissism usually occurs at the threshold of the problem of sexual difference, a problem that will find its resolution in the acceptance of castration, this hysterical strategy is adopted in an attempt to evade the question of having, the inevitable confrontation with lack.

The hysteric's phallic narcissism most often takes the spectacular and unmodulated form of "putting on a show," that is, of staging a performance in which his primary goal is to offer himself to the other's gaze as the embodiment of the ideal object of desire. The hysteric must therefore identify with this object bodily as well as through speech. The essential thing is to appear as a brilliant object that will fascinate the other.

All the seductive enterprises that the hysteric undertakes are based on this phallic brilliance. For it is the case that, in hysteria, seduction is always fundamentally in the service of the phallus more than it is in the service of desire. In other words, it is more important to reinforce the imaginary identification with the phallus than to desire the other. What must happen, against all odds, is to cause the other to desire, to make him desire this fascinating object that is displayed as the object that can satisfy his lack. But it is even more important to keep the other in suspense during this process. As long as the other is running after such an object, the hysteric can maintain the fantasy of his phallic identification. But, as we know, as soon as the other stops merely pursuing and actually wants to do something about his desire, he usually runs the risk of being shown the door. Hysterics are, in effect, masters at not getting what they want.

From the point of view of identification with the object of the other's lack, the problematic is one and the same for female and male hysterics, since the issue is the way one positions one-self with regard to castration. On the other hand, the neurotic strategies take different forms depending on the gender of the subject. For a woman, the relation to the aspect of having will be that of *not having it*, while for a man it will be that of *being presumed to have it*. This bifurcation in the register of having will lead to paths of realization that are typical for the gender of the subject in question. As we shall see in the following chapters, it is principally in connection with sex that we find distinctive profiles for feminine and masculine hysteria.

12

The Hysterical Woman and Sex

To the extent that it is based on desire, the relation to the other's genital is always desire for the phallus in the other. Thus a woman can find, in a man, what he does not entirely have. And, correspondingly, some phallic dimension projected onto the woman mobilizes a man's desire for her. In both cases each of the protagonists is presumed to have what the other does not have. In other words, it is the element of *lack* that governs the relationship to sex.

In a way, constituting oneself as being able to be the other's phallus always implies the refusal to encounter this lack, and this is the typical fantasmatic position of the hysteric. Conversely, the acknowledgment of lack always entails acknowledgment of the other's castration. Thus the circulation of desire between a man and a woman is crucially dependent on the mutual acknowledgment of castration in the other. For the man, this circulation begins when he presents himself to a woman under the aspect of "I don't have the phallus," for the woman, when she presents herself under the aspect of "I am not the phallus." We can therefore see right away why it is that the hysteric is involved in an impossibility when it comes to his relation to the other's sex, a symptomatic impossibility vouched for by his unfulfilled desire. This, in turn, stems from the fact that the hysteric never acknowledges these two manifestations of castration.

Let us look first at the relation to sex in female hysteria; in the following chapter masculine hysteria will be discussed.

This relation to sex is highly overdetermined by a number of elements in reality that serve as supports for the hysterical logic of desire. Although these reality-based supports are different, they are nevertheless chosen because their objective is the same: the ideal for which the hysteric spares no sacrificial effort. The hysterical woman is motivated by the endless concern for perfection in the name of this ideal. More precisely, what we are dealing with is a requirement with regard to perfection that is supported by certain cultural and ideological stereotypes, beginning with the notion that the beautiful and the feminine are intrinsically connected.

It is one thing to observe that the hysterical woman is constantly tormented by her concern for beauty, quite another thing to see how beauty comes to overlap with femininity to the point of supplanting it. Curiously enough, this concern for beauty in thrall to the ideal of perfection is usually expressed in negative self-evaluations: "I'm too this," "I've got too little of that," "I look awful," "My body should be like this," "My face should be like that," and so on.

At first glance, there is nothing very unusual in all this, since everyone's ordinary narcissism is put to the test on occasion. But for the hysteric, this testing assumes overwhelming proportions; for her, narcissism becomes an absolute. This is all the more true because one's personal fantasy system with regard to beauty is customarily bound up with the ways in which one wants to or is able to please others. Now, in itself this wish to please others by no means calls for a global demand for beauty, a perfection such that other people's evaluations of us would have the force of law. Although wanting to please involves getting a certain amount of attention from others, it does not have to reach for the utmost perfection in order to obtain this assurance.

But this is a distinction that the hysteric does not entirely grasp; there still remains the secret hope of attaining the heights of perfection. On this point the hysterical strategy is blind, that is, true to itself: to summon the other in such a way that he is completely fascinated and subjugated. Her mad enterprise amounts to persisting in the fantasy of an other who will be totally flabbergasted by the embodiment of such perfection. Fortunately, this never occurs with an other who acknowledges castration.

The hysteric is the harshest judge when it comes to the ascent to the ideal of perfection. Nothing can ever be beautiful enough to wipe out the traces of imperfections and faults. This despotic requirement inevitably causes symptoms to appear, of which the most striking is the hysteric's permanent indecision with regard to everything. Whether it is a question of the most ordinary, everyday matters or of more significant, long-term ones, we find the same symptomatic strategy at work in, for example, the choice of a garment, a pair of shoes, a brand of toothpaste, or, ultimately, a romantic partner. Although the process of choosing eventually comes to an end because of sheer exhaustion, what is chosen remains the object of uncertainty, doubts, and regrets. The ceaseless negotiations back and forth that result from this only increase the initial hesitation, since no object that has been chosen is capable of reassuring or of serving its function more adequately than one that was rejected.

It is on the level of choosing a romantic partner that this problem of hesitation becomes most acute. Here the hysteric suffers from having no criterion of assurance. Given the nature of the investment in question, she tortures herself to her heart's content in her love affairs. And in this area she actualizes some of the most characteristic features of the hysterical structure. "Being there without being there" is, in the hysteric's relation to the other, a useful escape hatch when it turns out that the wrong choice was made. This tendency is important in view of the economy of hysterical desire, the permanent feature of which is remaining unsatisfied.

In this sense, we might say that the diabolical search for perfection actually expresses its own negative—the permanent conviction that one is imperfect. We can therefore understand why the hysteric is on such easy terms with the aspect of make-believe, through which she attempts to mask the imperfections that she experiences as psychically overpowering. Anything and everything can serve as a mask: clothing, jewelry, role playing, ostentatious identifications. Everything can be put to use in order to make more attractive, to the gaze of the other, what is presumed to be so unattractive. This is the completely inauthentic side of the hysteric, the basis of her inconsistency and lability.

As part of the same phenomenon, the hysterical woman is as insecure about her moral and intellectual substance as she is about her physical perfection. Her flaws are never limited to what can be seen of her body; they extend to her intelligence and her mind, so that the "make believe" appears in this register as well, and with the same techniques of camouflage. Her favorite expression, "I'm so ignorant," reveals how burdened she is by the feeling that she can never be smart or cultured enough in the eyes of the other. This disposition can sometimes look like a real persecution complex as far as intelligence is concerned. Her constant lament is represented in symptomatic inhibitions with a familiar leitmotiv: "It's no use my reading books, since I never remember anything"; "I don't understand anything anyone explains to me"; and so on.

This connection to knowledge offers fertile ground for the painful actualization of imperfections; it is in fact much harder to repair intellectual flaws by the artifices or illusions that can cover over physical defects. And so there is no one like the hysteric for denouncing such artifices when they attempt to deceive in the realm of knowledge. She is the most merciless judge and censor: no lapse can be concealed. Since knowledge must be absolute, she subscribes without reservation to the fantasy that "either you know something, or, if you don't, you're totally ignorant." When one is unable to demonstrate that one knows everything, pretending that one nevertheless knows a little something thus seems to be a disgrace, even an imposture.

The hysteric therefore persuades herself from the outset that she will never master the least bit of knowledge. In these circumstances she resorts to "make-believe," trying desperately to be the reflection of the knowledge of an other. To gain access to other people's thought, she undertakes to become its unconditional support through imaginary adhesion, thereby making herself into its pure and simple echo. Once again we see here that structural feature of hysteria that consists in being there without truly being on the side of one's own desire. By making herself the mouthpiece of another's knowledge, she overcomes her own deficits. Being a "megaphone" in this way entails the constant concern to please the other and to set herself up as the object that can fill his lack. To please the other, she first has to think like him, then to speak like him, and—in the best-case scenario, if she finds favorable conditions—to think and speak like him, but in his place. This insubstantiality is in accord with the project of dissolving in the other's desire and thus existing merely as his reflection.

In this disposition we find the privileged servitude in which the hysteric places herself with regard to the one chosen for the role of Master, the one who is established, in advance, as he who is unable not to know everything. The hysteric strives to become the reflection of his thought, and hysterical discourse, therefore, characteristically becomes the discourse of an other's discourse. In this sense, being borrowed, it can be everyone's discourse.

The unconditional adherence to perfection brings to the fore another characteristic manifestation of hysteria: the problem of *identification with the woman* that torments every hysteric to the extent that the question of her feminine identity comes into play. It is a commonplace that the hysteric always fixes on one or another feminine model as she tries to assume her own femininity. Historically, we may recall the case of Dora (Freud 1905b), who was captivated by the qualities and charms of Mrs. K. Freud was quick to sense, in the vicissitudes of this identificatory process, one of the most fundamental constants of hysterical functioning. It is in this dimension that we find the emergence and unfolding of hysterical homosexuality, which is bound up more with the process of identification than with the choice of a love object.

If the hysteric is so easily enthralled by another woman taken as a model, it is because this other woman is presumed to hold the answer to that question that is so crucial for the hysteric: What is it to be a woman? It is because of this central issue that hysterical homosexuality is not concerned with choosing a woman as an ideal love object. On the contrary, in her homosexual promiscuity the hysteric is above all seeking to be like her, to think like her, to live like her, to make love like her, to have the same men, and so on. In other words, what is happening here is that the hysteric is basically vampirizing the other woman who, she assumes, has brought her feminine identity to a state of perfection.

This vampirizing of the feminine model allows us to understand certain aspects of the relationships of female hysterics to couples. Completing the appropriation of the feminine model involves, at a minimum, entirely sharing her choices and her tastes. So with just one step further she goes on to steal the other woman's romantic partners. Experience shows how readily some hysterics entice away their friends' male partners, and all the more so because the other woman's partner is always "better equipped" than her own. The question of making the right choice comes back again—the other man always has something more, something better, than her current one. The other man is just like the garment or the shoes she didn't select; he turns out to be infinitely more satisfactory than the one she decided on. And so what follows is the same scenario, the same lament, and the same disillusionment.

It is in the choice of a love partner that the hysterical woman will sustain her adherence to the ideal of perfection as long as she possibly can. This is why defiance plays such an essential role. The hysteric tries to get the man who is guaranteed in advance to respond to all her demands. In this strategy she unknowingly fails to realize that this is the way never to meet any man who can rise to the occasion. Hence the excessive tendency of certain hysterical women to choose an unattainable partner; the further out of reach he is, the longer she can sustain the illusion that the object of her love will not be disappointing.

This explains the tendency of hysterics to fix their choice on a partner who is a "stranger," not only in the usual sense of the term but especially in view of his nature as radically "other." The more alien he is, the longer he can fill the imaginary role of the unattainable partner. If, in addition, he is a stranger in reality, at a significant and more or less permanent distance from the hysteric, he then becomes the partner of her dreams. On the other hand, as soon as the "stranger" returns to everyday life in the here and now, his ideal qualities take a nosedive, and he at once becomes as disappointing as all the others. This is the origin of the much-cherished hysterical fantasy of being, say, the wife of a transoceanic seaman ("It's wonderful, because it's so great when you get together again!") or the girlfriend of an engineer who has to spend much of the year at the bottom of the Antarctic. These particular scenarios may not be common, but we can imagine a whole series of variations on the general theme. The hysterical woman may find a more practical solution, protecting the imaginary representation of the ideal man by choosing as a romantic partner someone who is involved in another relationship. Such a man appears to be the only one for her precisely because he belongs to another woman. The hysteric can then be upset because, of all men, the only one she is interested in is out of reach.

In these various tribulations that the hysteric undergoes with regard to her romantic partners we can observe a particular constant: her mute—or, instead, bizarre—complaint against men. Everything that might serve as a criterion of selection is turned into its opposite. Nevertheless, there is one area in which the meaning of the hysterical lament becomes clear, and that is the sexual criterion. Consciously or not, the hysterical woman maintains a special vigilance concerning sexual performance. Whether that performance is positive or negative is unimportant. What matters above all is that sexuality must become the object of a discourse of claim or demand. Thus the hysteric can always be envious of another woman's man on the grounds that he is more potent, more skilled, even more tireless. But her complaint can just as well refer to a less exalted set of criteria.

Such a claim functions all the better because it usually finds some warrant on the male side; the phallic competition of hysterical women reinforces the masculine striving for virility. On the one hand, we have the characteristic hysterical demands: "He doesn't know how to bring me to orgasm"; "He doesn't want to make love often enough"; "His penis is too big"; or, as the case may be, "too small." On the other hand, we note the masculine sensitivity aroused by these demands that call phallic potency into question. Made anxious on the level of his male fantasies, the man overdoes on the level of performance. In this tragic competition, pathetic misunderstandings reach their height, since the man, challenged in his virility, is eager to prove that he is not impotent. The hysteric can then take advantage of her partner's renewed efforts by, as one might expect, making them a new source of disappointment: "He always wants to make love, without even asking whether I'm in the mood."

In these cruel exchanges, if the hysterical woman does not know what she is really demanding through her sexual complaint, we must admit that her male partner is equally blind in his total misrecognition of what a woman wants from him. The hysteric who complains of being unsatisfied sexually has, most often unconsciously, adopted a masculine position. She belongs to the imaginary universe of phallic competition. Her sexual complaint bears direct witness to the illusory criteria of sexual strength or weakness that men have created for themselves with regard to the ideal of virile perfection. In fact, men who are unknowingly caught up in the fear of sexual failure or inadequacy are often led to assume an attitude of artifice and "make-believe" toward any reproach that a woman might make to them in this matter. Women are quite familiar with the tricks, the lies, and the laborious precautions that men resort to in order to avoid being confronted by such an assault on their narcissism.

If the sexual claim of the hysteric has this profile, it is because it is sure to strike an appropriately responsive chord in men. The more the hysteric complains of being sexually dissatisfied, the more she mobilizes men's sexual dissatisfaction. Conversely, the more blindly confident the man is sexually, the more he proves, by his performance, that the hysteric has good reason to keep on expecting more from him. We are familiar with this tragicomic "dialogue of the deaf" that is so wearing for the combatants. In short, the hysteric sustains this kind of claim only because it puts to the test her certainty that she is dissatisfied.

The hysterical woman cannot fix her choice on the first man she meets, in that this choice must always be potentially able to be undone. It is always, or almost always, accompanied by tentativeness, by trial and error, all of which is well suited to keeping the hysterical hesitation going. The boyfriend is usually chosen merely because he comes along after a disappointment or the breakup of a relationship. The hysteric gives him to understand that she chose him on the rebound, that he is a secondhand partner. Here we come upon the psychic paradox that underlies the hysteric's desire in her relation to the other. The "chosen one" achieves his position only because of the demands for perfection that trap him in a relationship of privileged investment. But, as it turns out, he is divested of this privilege in advance, at least in the sense that the hysteric indicates to him that he is taking the place of another man who mattered a lot to her, of an unattainable other who would have been more suitable. Such a partner is thus always chosen for lack of anything better.

In this problematic, the body becomes a priority for the hysteric. She "gives" her body ("I gave myself to him"). This imaginary dimension of the gift leads to the sacrificial position of the hysteric, which is largely sustained by today's sociocultural phallic ideology. From the vantage point of this ideology, the hysterical woman appears imaginarily as the one through whom the man can come into being, the one through whom the man's incompleteness can find the most perfect possible object of fulfillment. It is not surprising that the hysteric chooses "the man of importance," that is, the man for whom she can feel indispensable in shoring up something of this very importance: "If it weren't for me . . ."; "Without me you'd be nothing"; and so on.

On this point I want to be more precise about the special nature of the imaginary connection between the "man of importance" and the hysteric's father. It is a common error to believe that the hysteric is always seeking a man who is the substitute for a paternal image. The man who is sought—and possibly found—is never a simple replica of the father. What the hysteric is looking for in a man is a *complete father*, that is, a father who never existed. Through the choice of a male partner she wants, above all, to make up for the imaginary deficiencies of the father. She is willing to attribute to him everything the father lacked—he must be stronger, handsomer, more potent, and so on, than her father was. And it is in this sense, and only in this sense, that such a man can be the Master that the hysteric is seeking.

The prostitution fantasy found so often in hysterics is constituted around this issue. This is not the fantasy of the sacrificial position toward all men, since it concerns only one. The prostitute can *sell* herself to all men only insofar as she conforms strictly to the fantasmatic myth that she can *give* herself to only one man, to the pimp who is in the position of mastery. He is the "master of bodies," but not for any arbitrary reason. It is not because of his mastery of technique or any special ability to possess women and give them sexual pleasure. The hysterical fantasy of prostitution draws its energy from the fact that the "master of bodies" is the one *who is lacking*. This is why the prostitute pays him. He needs her and her money to be complete. And the more she pays, the more she invests him as complete. It is for this reason, incidentally, that this fantasy is so easily mobilized in the context of the psychoanalytic situation.

We have here an entirely characteristic subjective position of the hysteric with regard to a man insofar as there is some lack in him. This position differs from the relation to the other, as described above, in which the hysteric offers her perfection to a Master who is presumed to be as perfect as she is. As soon as this "offering" reaches a certain magnitude, we are very close to a psychotic position. In fact, the conviction of having what the other lacks has only to become a real certainty for the hysteric to become destabilized in a transient delusional episode. If this happens rarely, it is because the Master never truly occupies the place that the hysteric assigns to him. He falls from the heights and quickly proves to be a disappointment. And then, no longer possessing the ideal qualifications that the hysteric had conferred upon him, he becomes merely an object of dissatisfaction.

13

Masculine Hysteria

Masculine hysteria has a different origin, but as a psychic structure this neurosis concerns men as well as women. Hysteria in men is clearly reinforced by dissimulation on the part of doctors where diagnosis is concerned. The medical profession is very resistant to identifying hysteria in a man, and the neurosis is therefore camouflaged in a number of ways. Among these artifices we often find the search for a cause outside the symptom, the emphasis on a respectable reason. It seems important to attribute to others, or to the external environment, what exists within oneself alone. We can therefore understand why one of the causal factors most frequently invoked to protect this disguise is traumatization.

If the psychically resonant trauma has the least association with a physical one, hysteria in men is masked even further. Consider, for example, work-related accidents, even acts of war, and we have at our disposal formal clinical categories to conceal the etiology of the symptoms. Nosological entities such as "post-traumatic disorders" and "war neuroses" reveal the deceptiveness of this masquerade. To exorcise the guilt hinted at by the symptom we can distort the clinical picture by some official recognition—sick benefits, pensions, even some honorary titles—and then masculine hysteria, recognized, recompensed, decorated, can be flaunted all the better because social respectability is the surest way for it to avoid having its triumphant neurotic workings brought to light.

To be sure, not all cases of masculine hysteria avail themselves of such disguises. But the insistence with which some men parade the psychic repercussions of their traumas suggests hysteria, especially when these traumas have no direct connection with the characteristic physical sequelae.

From the point of view of clinical symptomatology there is no reason to distinguish masculine hysteria from the feminine kind. At most, we find it defined differently, in the terms of reference of a medical discourse that emasculates the imaginary excesses usually ascribed to the overwhelming expression of hysteria in women. Masculine hysteria does not have the advantage of thirty-five centuries of history behind it! For example, major hysterical crises seem all but nonexistent in the context of masculine hysteria. What we find are less spectacular manifestations such as feelings of being unwell, lipothymias, or vague, diffuse states of fatigue.

There is, however, a symptom of masculine hysteria that metaphorically recalls the "major crisis," and this is the fit of rage (see Chapter 9). These outbursts are often said to be caused by frustration. The frustrations in question usually seem to be the minor, ordinary, inevitable stresses of daily life, but they are expressed in a self-damaging way that calls attention to a malaise that can be reduced only through psychic discharge in a fit of rage. In other words, the angry outburst amounts to a *confession of impotence* that disguises a libidinal discharge.

Although we do not find in men certain typical expressions of feminine hysteria (anesthesia, paralysis, spasms, sensory disorders), we can identify certain types of bodily fear that are sometimes reminiscent of hypochondria: fear of heart disease with all its prodromal symptoms, joint diseases, various digestive disturbances, poorly defined neurovegetative disorders, and so on. On the other hand, the ordinary share of multiple conversion pains are found just as often in men as in women, and the way they are elaborated psychically and disguised symptomatically is similar in both sexes.

For example, what was described earlier as the concern that one be seen or heard is entirely evident in masculine hysteria. Nevertheless, the "showing" of the hysterical woman pertains to some part of her body, whereas for the man it refers to his body as a whole. What is essentially in question in this showing of oneself is the desire to be seen, the desire to please—when all is said and done, a demand for love and recognition. This explains the basic tendency to seduction in male hysteria. The man shows "himself" as such, more than he shows anything else. Hence we find the inevitable self-confident behavior, in which artifice is used every bit as much as it is by the hysterical woman. In masculine hysteria, seduction is the mainstay in the conduct of a love affair; in order to make sure that he is universally loved, the male hysteric offers his own love without letting up on himself. These are, of course, bogus relationships, in that he is incapable of getting involved on a level beyond seduction. Since he cannot give anyone up, or lose any possible love object, he is above all bent on being loved by everyone. Here we have one of the major components of hysteria, dissatisfaction.

In pursuit of his romantic strategy, the male hysteric divides himself among several people with whom he easily becomes involved at the same time. This is the permanent state of hesitation that we have observed in other aspects of the hysteric's life—choosing a career or a romantic partner, making an important decision, and so on. It is always the interest that someone else takes in an object that makes it the object desired by the hysterical man; thus we find the potential victim stance that leaves him susceptible to all sorts of suggestion. Conversely, the hysteric develops a permanent regret that he cannot derive any benefit from what he has: "The other person's career would have suited me better"; "The other person's wife would surely have been more satisfying, since she's more desirable"; "It's the garment I didn't buy that would have been the most appropriate"; and so on. One might say that the hysterical man's motto is that he cannot take pleasure in, or profit from, what he has but always regrets what he doesn't have.

And yet if he somehow manages to obtain what he doesn't have, things will turn out badly, since his strategy is to sustain dissatisfaction. This is a structural feature peculiar to masculine hysteria: failure or self-defeating behavior. When the hysteric gets what he had coveted when it belonged to the other, he does not rest until he has failed. The realm of professional activity is especially well suited to this purpose, since failures can come about in a quite spectacular way as the man becomes the victim exposed to the gaze of all.

We have a very specific terminology to designate what, in the end, is just a trait of hysterical structure: failure neurosis or fate neurosis.

Failure neurosis is a nosographic category introduced by René Laforgue (1939) to highlight the psychic configuration in which subjects turn out to be the architects of their own misfortune, in the sense that they are apparently unable to bear the achievement of what they seem to desire the most. This is failure in the face of success—it is as if success triggered a mechanism of self-punishment so that the satisfaction is rejected. This compulsion to repeat failure brings to mind what Freud (1920) called fate neurosis, a symptomatic strategy in which we see the repeated return of a series of dramatic events. But this repetition is such that the subject can deceive himself about his own personal involvement: "It's a blow of fate"; "Destiny strikes once again." As Freud so astutely observed, this life of failure is crafted in advance by the subject, but in such a way that the repetition of unconscious determinants always takes on the appearance of unforeseeable external events.

There are certain palliatives, certain processes of overcompensation in this failure syndrome. For the most part, the failure in the face of success becomes established when two series of incompatible elements coincide. On the one hand, there is a tendency on the part of the hysteric to refer in an obvious way to his own ambitions, his talents, his potential for success, and on the other a tendency toward victimization that ascribes to external reality the failure to realize the first set of qualities. In other words, the indication or the element that would support the subject's advancement seems to act as a signal that mobilizes the repetition compulsion. As soon as the hysteric is assured that his desire can potentially be fulfilled, he renders himself unfit to achieve it. The result is the establishment of states of anxiety, depression, even neurasthenia, identical to those found in feminine hysteria. It is on the basis of this incapacity, unconsciously orchestrated by the hysteric, that there evolves an elaborate system of overcompensations, the two most frequent manifestations of which are alcoholism and drug use. (This does not mean, however, that all alcoholics and drug addicts are hysterics.)

It is important to understand the precise function of these addictions in the context of masculine hysteria. Alcohol and drugs provide a compensatory element for the hysteric in his sense of himself as a man, as we shall see in the next chapter in which his sexual relation to the other is examined. The hysteric has to try to seem "like a man" exactly at the point where, as he laments, he can never manage to do so. The toxic substance serves as a mediator, allowing him to throw the other—man or woman—off the scent. With a woman, it enables him to cultivate the illusion that he indeed possesses what he thinks she expects from him, namely the phallic object. With a man, it makes it possible for him, in a way that is just as illusory, to present himself as a potential rival, that is, as his equal, since the other man is presumed to have what the hysteric complains that he himself lacks. In both cases we observe the ambivalence underlying the hysteric's sexual problematics, that is to say, the ambivalence between living for oneself and being seen in the gaze of the other, or, to put it differently, between desiring for oneself and desiring, despite oneself, on the basis of one's assessment of what the other supposedly expects from the standpoint of *his* desire.

14

The Male Hysteric and Sex

The sexual problematics of the hysterical man have to do with that aspect of the relation to the other in which the subject strives to please everyone. But the relation to the feminine other is, from the outset, alienated in a representation of the woman as idealized and inaccessible (see Chapter 9). This frequently leads to the development of modes of conduct designed to avoid a direct personal confrontation with the woman in the area of sex.

The result is the institution of perverse behaviors, of which one of the most common is the homosexual mask or game. This is not a true homosexuality based on the choice of an exclusively male love object. What we have here is at most a homosexual parody that serves to provide the reassurance of secondary compensations. Since the other is similar to one, he offers protection from sexual difference. This is not to say that the feminine is necessarily absent from the concerns of the hysterical man. On the contrary, it is quite present, but it is tolerable insofar as it is mediated in this way. The male hysteric's homosexuality often entails compulsive masturbation accompanied by fantasies with a perverse connotation, among others erotic scenarios involving lesbians.

Exhibitionism is another perverse manifestation often deployed by the male hysteric as a presentation of his body (and not as the uncovering of his genitals as is the case with true perversions). By means of this exhibitionism the hysteric repeats something of the provocative theatricality of the homosexual parody. Since make-believe is always sustained by the gaze of the other, it enables the subject to enjoy, in fantasy, the supposedly disapproving or hostile opinion the other has of him. If the other lends himself at all to this imaginary capture, the *jouissance* is optimal. In fact, every scandal, every denunciation or arrest, every charge brought against him is one more piece of evidence proving that the deceptive scenario has functioned well (see Dor 1989).

In addition to this perverse camouflage designed to keep the feminine object at a distance, the hysteric frequently resorts to another symptomatic expression, impotence, which has the additional advantage of reinforcing his compulsion to fail. Whether this impotence is total or occurs in the aborted form of premature ejaculation, it is based on the same imaginary mechanism in which the subject confuses desire and virility.

This confusion stems from a particular interpretation that the hysteric develops with regard to a woman's request. He never perceives such a request as a desirous appeal directed to a man's desire; on the contrary, he perceives it as an injunction that requires him to prove his manhood. In other words, it is as if a relationship of desire entailed the necessity to demonstrate that he really "has" what the woman is asking for, namely the phallus. Since the male hysteric does not feel that he possesses such an object, he accordingly replies to the woman, "I don't have a penis," whence his impotence. Thus the confusion between desire and virility reveals a confusion about the nature of this object, a confusion between the phallus and the organ. In the hysterical man's economy of desire, having a penis logically implies having the phallus.

One of the most typical examples of this problematic is the figure of the playboy. For most of these men, oddly enough, each initial encounter with a new woman ends up with their being impotent. But this is not as puzzling as it might at first seem, once we discover the unconscious mechanisms at work in the playboy, mechanisms that produce the conjunction of symptomatic features leading to impotence. First, his unconscious relationship with his mother is fraught with significance. From this perspective we may consider impotence to be a reply to the mother's unconscious demand: he is still attached to her. Hence he leaves himself open to numerous experiences in which complete or partial sexual failure bears witness to the fact that his mother is the only woman who can mobilize his desire.

This is another way of indicating that the hysteric does not have the phallus, at least to the extent that his mother gave him to understand that *she* might possibly have it. And, in addition, she gave him to understand that he *was* it. We have here a common phallic configuration in which, as a child, a man was put in the position of making up for his mother's lack. Impotence thus becomes a compromise between giving a woman pleasure (this is the phallic test supposedly required by the woman) and remaining faithful to mother by presenting himself to a woman as an object of representation and not an object of possible consummation.

In reality, this process is manifested in the playboy's permanent obsession with "having" one woman after another ("See that woman over there? I'll have her."). The woman is invested as a trophy that enables the hysteric, in an ostentatious show of virility, to keep up a rivalry with other men, those other men who, he is sure, have the phallus.

There is still another form of this hysterical position associated with impotence, namely body-building. The body-builder is in a state of permanent representation of the phallus; because he does not have the phallus itself, he indicates metaphorically, with his body, that he *is* it. Here the confusion between penis and phallus is a different one. The penis is imaginarily represented by the whole body, whence the need to prove, to confirm over and over again, the strength of the muscles. Exercising the muscles stands metaphorically for erection, which is most often annoyingly absent in such subjects. The phallic fantasy is thus organized in this peculiar way: since she has no penis of her own to give her pleasure, a woman can always enjoy this muscle-penis as she gazes on him. The exaggerated exhibitionism of body-builders can thus be explained by the fact that the showing off of the body in one competition after another is never anything but a contest of penile erection.

Premature ejaculation is a related phenomenon, although it stems from a psychic process somewhat different from the one involved in impotence. It points to an imaginary danger in the sex act with a woman; although such an act is possible, it entails a risk, the risk of not being able to prove to the woman that the man really has the phallus and can therefore undertake the act to the full extent. This end point is always the same: a woman cannot experience pleasure unless the man demonstrates his phallic mastery to her. It is easy to see why this imaginary performance causes such anxiety. Anxiety both precipitates and short-circuits the process. The expected goal, which is especially threatening, is feminine *jouissance*. For the male hysteric, only the one who is the absolute master of the phallus can take on feminine *jouissance*, that is, dominate it. The woman's *jouissance* is, in effect, always perceived as a defeat in the face of triumphant phallic power. Not having the attribute that would enable him to bring off this victory, the hysteric can only feel that he himself is subjected to the power of the one who has it. Unconsciously he is trapped in the imaginary dimension of surrender to this phallic power. In addition, he unconsciously identifies with his female partner, and the orgasmic pleasure of his premature ejaculation is what he imagines a woman's orgasm to be like as she succumbs to phallic power. The more he assures himself that a woman's *jouissance* cannot resist phallic power, the more he assumes the position of the one who does not have the phallus, and the more he experiences premature orgasm.

In such men we find a significant fantasy construction: "real manly men." These are men who bring a woman to orgasm the moment they enter her, supermen who can bring all women to orgasm, who settle the score with all frigid women, who give women multiple orgasms and make them beg for mercy, beg the man to stop as they swoon with sexual pleasure. . . .

Part IV

The Obsessional Structure

15

The Problematics
of Obsessional Neurosis

As was the case with the perversions and hysteria, I want to begin the discussion of obsessional structure with a consideration of the way in which the subject actualizes his desire with regard to the phallic function. Obsessional structure is not a psychic organization found only in men. Although it is much more rare in women, it occurs among them as well, with the same panoply of characteristic symptomatic manifestations. But to be concise, I shall be examining obsessional neurosis only in men.

Psychoanalytic tradition often presents obsessional structure as a psychic organization that is distinctively opposed to hysterical organization in a number of ways. Although this is a convenient perspective, it is an ambiguous one, since such a contrast is not only relative but also quite inadequate. It is based merely on some phenomenological observations and not on structural features.

The main point of such observations is to stress a specific element that might make the contrast more plausible: unlike the hysteric, the obsessional feels that his mother loved him too much. Although this unquestionably appears to be the case, it in no way provides grounds for a facile contrast between obsessionality and hysteria, as is demonstrated by the fact that this is a situational element that we often observe in perverse organizations as well. From the diagnostic point of view we cannot rely on this observational factor.

Nevertheless, we do have here a valuable component of obsessional logic. To emphasize that the obsessional felt that he was excessively loved by his mother is to mark out something specific about the phallic function. The obsessional does in fact often present as a subject who was heavily invested phallically as the privileged object of maternal desire. This is why, as we have seen, the obsessional is said to be nostalgic for the state of *being* the phallus. This longing is primarily supported by the memory of the particular kind of relationship that the obsessional had with his mother—or, more precisely, the kind of relationship she had with him. We always find, in the history of obsessionals, a child who was his mother's favorite, or at any rate one who, at a given moment, could feel that he was in a privileged position with regard to her.

Given the stakes of desire involved in the phallic logic, this "privilege" necessarily leads the child to develop a strong premature notion of himself as the object in whom the mother will find what she is not able to get from the father. We are here at one of the turning points of the oedipal dialectic, the passage from *being* to *having* the phallus, in which the mother appears to the child to be dependent on the father insofar as the father establishes the law of her desire. This is, of course, a psychic experience that the child senses and interprets. If the father presumably lays down the law for the mother, this happens only if the mother herself presumably desires what she does not have and what the father possesses.

What is in question is the *symbolic investment* of the father that ends in the attribution of the phallus to him. The passage from *being* to *having* the phallus is always made through this displacement of the phallic attribute, and such a displacement can come about only to the extent that something important has been signified to the child in the maternal discourse, namely that the object of her desire is clearly dependent on the person of the father. Only the meaning of such dependence can get the child moving toward the dimension of *having* the phallus. If the discourse of the mother communicates certain ambiguities with regard to the localization of the object of her desire, the child can then establish himself in a system in which it is he who completes the fulfillment of that desire. This is a crucial point in the formation of obsessional structure.

What is at issue is not, strictly speaking, a standing-in for the object of the mother's desire. If that were the case, we would be dealing with determinants of the organization of the perversions, or even the psychoses. The question here is rather one of supplementing what is missing in the satisfaction of the mother's desire, which presupposes that this satisfaction was clearly represented to the child as lacking. The above-mentioned ambiguity lies precisely in this dependence of the mother's desire concerning the father. What the mother indicates to the child, out of his awareness, can be summarized in two elements that do not entirely overlap. On the one hand, the child is well aware that the mother is dependent on the father when it comes to her desire; but, on the other hand, she does not seem to be getting from the father everything she presumably expects from him. When the child perceives this gap in maternal satisfaction, he sees the way clear to providing a supplement.

The child, then, is confronted with the law of the father, but he is captivated by the message of maternal dissatisfaction.

On this last point, it should be noted that, in the child's eyes, the mother does not seem radically unsatisfied. There is at most a partial emptiness in her satisfaction that the mother will try to fill by seeking a possible complement in the child. It is in this sense, and only in this sense, that the obsessional is the object of a special investment that leads him to believe that he is the preferred, privileged child. But I want to repeat that this privilege is never anything other than making up for the deficient satisfaction of the mother. Even though the child is logically led to the law of the father by the maternal discourse that inscribes her desire there, this supplementation is nonetheless conducive to the persistence of a phallic identification. And so the obsessional will always feel a pull toward a regressive return to such an identification at the same time as he obeys the paternal law and what it entails.

Although this return to *being* the phallus is actively wished for in order to fill the lack indicated in the maternal discourse, it is never fully accomplished. It is only through the symptomatic nostalgia that we can see certain characteristic structural traits of the obsessional economy of desire. Similarly, because the recognition of the symbolic father is based on certain ambiguities, it too leads to some striking manifestations. As we shall see, the ongoing nostalgic pull is illustrated, among other ways, by the *flight forward* that the obsessional constantly enacts with regard to his desire.

16

Features of the Obsessional Structure

We can now begin to look in more detail at the structural characteristics of obsessional neurosis and hence at the way they can be distinguished from matters of symptomatology. In particular, we can isolate structural traits that determine the course of desire. Consider the imperiousness of the necessity and duty that surround the obsessional organization of pleasure, along with weakness of demand and ambivalence as other traits associated with symptomatic defenses such as obsessional ideation; isolation and undoing; ritualization; reaction formation; the triad of guilt, mortification, and contrition; and the rest of the clinical picture of what, following Freud, is customarily called the anal character.

Let us start at the point where obsessional neurosis is formed—the sign of the mother's unsatisfied desire, through which the child joins her in the particular privileged dual relationship discussed above. Early on, the child perceives the signs of this dissatisfaction. The substrate of erotic investments that usually underlies the so-called dyadic relationship lends itself all the more readily to the communication of this message because the relationship develops primarily in the area of satisfaction of needs and the physical care of the child; it therefore involves the access to the child's body that leads to erotic pleasure—*jouissance.*

Since such *jouissance* is an inevitable part of the mother–child relationship, the mother's libidinal economy can serve as a catalyst in such a way that the incomplete satisfaction of her desire becomes a determining factor for the child. Here we may recall Freud's account of the sexual etiology of obsessional neurosis. One of the initial aspects of this approach to neurosis was the seduction theory, originally presented as playing a major role in the general psychoanalytic view of neurosis. Soon, however, Freud began to ascribe a considerably smaller influence to seduction, in apparent recantation of his original position.[1] Yet this was not a true abandonment of the earlier view. At most, what Freud renounced was the belief in the systematic importance of seduction as the cause of neurosis; in other words, seduction was to play a lesser role.[2]

Thus if we cannot continue to think of seduction as a constitutive cause of obsessional neurosis, it is nonetheless a predisposing element. We should keep in mind that, historically, Freud described the characteristics of obsessionality and hysteria at the same time, classifying obsessional pathology among the defense neuroses and highlighting the fact that in this type of neurosis defensive processes are predominant among symptomatic manifestations. As far as obsessional neurosis is concerned, then, Freud introduces the theme of seduction in a way that is entirely typical for him. Obsessions are held to be disguised reproaches that the subject addresses to himself in con-

---

1. See the letter written to Fliess on September 21, 1897 (Freud 1954).

2. For a detailed account of the seduction theory and its place in Freud's thought, see Laplanche and Pontalis 1973, pp. 404–408.

nection with infantile sexual activity that produced pleasure. Yet what makes the symptoms specifically obsessional is the way in which this childhood sexual activity was inscribed in relation to the mother's desire. According to Freud (1896), what took place was sexual aggression following a phase of seduction. As a result, libidinal drive impulses return in a disguised form— especially, in this case, as obsessional representations and affects. These elements are never anything more than primary defensive symptoms against which the ego reacts by mobilizing specific secondary defensive processes, among which isolation and un-doing, which we shall discuss further on, are predominant.

If seduction is not a prime etiological factor, therefore, it still plays a certain role in the relationship between mother and child. What Freud had intuited about maternal seduction does seem to be a determinative influence when we specify its im-pact as consisting in her signifying to the child, early on, that her desire is incompletely satisfied. As we shall see, it is the signifier of this insufficiency that will cause the child to have a particular psychic experience that feels like a seduction.

In this relational configuration it is, obviously, the mother who stimulates and sustains the child's erotic pleasure in the course of attending to his bodily needs. The child cannot help being the passive object of a seduction. Should he then be held captive in this *jouissance* because the insufficiency of the satis-faction of the mother's desire has been signified to him, this passive seduction is intensified and the resulting *jouissance* is experienced as sexual aggression. The child has no choice but to experience pleasure as a participant in his mother's privileged *jouissance*.

The surplus of love that we find in all obsessional subjects has its origin in this seduction, in which the mother appeals to the child to supply what is missing in her satisfaction. The child is called upon to somehow hold in abeyance the deficiency of maternal *jouissance*, and this gives rise to the sexual passivity that is so clearly in evidence in the elaborate daily fantasy productions of male obsessionals. In most of these men, it turns out, we find the nostalgic traces of this passive-aggressive seduction expressed in the common fantasy of being seduced by a woman without his active involvement, or even of being raped by a woman. A caricature of this fantasy takes the form of the "nurse" who is sexually aroused by stimulating her "patient" in the course of taking care of him.

This passivity with regard to sexual pleasure is one of the most characteristic features of the obsessional structure through which the subject nostalgically evokes his phallic identification. It is, in fact, with this passive phallic liability that the child destined to be an obsessional undertakes the crucial transition from *being* to *having* the phallus. And it is for this reason that gaining access to the realm of desire and the law is problematical for him, as is revealed by the nature of his relationship with his father and, beyond the father, with any authority figure who reactivates the paternal image.

The child necessarily experiences the passage from *being* to *having* as problematical because he has been thwarted in his phallic identification with the intruding father. We can easily understand why this transition is an especially difficult hurdle for the future obsessional. In the very place where he would normally come up against frustration, he is the captive of satisfaction in the relationship of supplementation that he maintains with his mother. Later on the obsessional will recall again and again how great a handicap this precocious but privileged experience of pleasure with his mother has been in the economy of his desire.

The premature capture by the mother does not allow the child to mediate his desire for himself. He remains, in effect, a prisoner of his mother's unfulfilled desire. More precisely, it is the child's desire for her that will, in return, kindle his own unfulfilled desire when he subsequently has the opportunity to make up for its lack. As a result, the entire process of desire is short-circuited for the child.

The dynamics of desire usually evolve in a threefold rhythm: *desire* separates out from *need* and then enters into *demand*. In the present case, as soon as desire separates out from need it is immediately taken up by the unfulfilled mother who sees in it a possible source of compensation. The distinctive profile of obsessional desire can be accounted for by the haste with which the mother thereby takes charge. The result is that the child's desire always bears the mark of urgent and imperative need, since when it first arose the mother did not allow it the time to remain suspended until a demand could be articulated.

This leads to the formation of two basic structural traits. On the one hand, obsessional neurosis always bears the mark of imperious need. On the other hand, the obsessional is stricken with weakness in the expression of his demand. His familiar masochistic passivity is largely the result of his finding it impossible to make a demand. He therefore tries to make the other guess at and articulate what he himself desires but can never manage to ask for. More generally, this weakness is part of the involuntary servitude in which the obsessional so readily confines himself. The inability to formulate a demand leads, paradoxically, to the *duty* to accept and endure everything. He feels constrained to accept all the consequences of his inability to demand, and does so mainly by occupying the place of the object of the other's *jouissance*. This passive attitude is an invitation to sadistic mistreatment at the hands of the other.

It is the obsessional's ongoing complaints about mistreatment that enable him to come to terms with his own deadly symptomatic *jouissance*. Signs of this *jouissance* appear clearly in reactive forms, the essential nature of which is laborious brooding on adversity. The underlying reason for this is that the obsessional's tendency to transform himself into the object of the other's *jouissance* reenacts the infantile situation in which he was confined in his phallic role as his mother's privileged child. This childhood scenario gives rise to the typical symptom of guilt stemming from the special, quasi-incestuous relationship to the mother in the context of castration. Because of this erotic fixation on the mother, the obsessional is always acutely fearful of castration; what is at issue, of course, is symbolic castration, and, as we shall see, the fear of it is expressed most strikingly in connection with the problematics of loss and the relation to the Law of the Father.

17

The Obsessional, Loss, and the Law of the Father

The obsessional is completely unable to tolerate loss. This is overwhelmingly evident in all aspects of daily life; just as he is inclined to constitute himself as *everything* for the other, so he must despotically control and master *everything* so that the other can in no way escape him—that is, so that he will lose nothing of the other. The loss of some element of the object cannot help reminding him of castration, of a defect in his narcissistic image. Conversely, to outdo castration is to try to win and maintain a phallic status with the mother and, more generally, any woman. And yet, because the Law of the Father is always present on the obsessional's horizon of desire, his guilt cannot be assuaged. It is this ambivalence between phallic nostalgia and the loss entailed in castration that places the obsessional in a specific structural position with regard to the father.

Since the paternal imago is omnipresent, it inevitably evokes the rivalry and competitiveness so dear to obsessionals. They constantly strive to take the place of the father (or of any figure who might represent him), which makes it absolutely necessary

to "kill" him in order to supplant him with mother. These archaic death wishes reappear in a more or less permanent way,
and always with the same pattern: taking the place of the other
who is unconsciously invested as a potential representative of
the symbolic father.

This concern to take the other's place leads the obsessional
to all sorts of struggles for prestige, and to grandiose and painful combats. Such clashes serve to reassure him of the saving
grace of castration; even though the Master is intolerable to him
insofar as he supposedly possesses what the obsessional covets,
he must be seen to be the Master and must remain so. As we
saw in Chapter 6, it is in this area that certain defiant behaviors
can be observed. Nevertheless, although the obsessional *needs*
to encounter a Master, this is not the same situation as with the
hysteric, who *seeks* one. Hysterical defiance of the Master is
always aimed at dethroning him, whereas for the obsessional the
Master must remain in place come what may. This is the goal of
all his competitiveness, for to try to take the Master's place is to
struggle to assure oneself that this coveted place is off limits, in
other words that the father cannot be supplanted. The Master
who cannot be overthrown thus continues, metaphorically, to
forbid and condemn the incestuous erotization of the relationship to the mother in which the obsessional is held captive.

Still, it remains the case that putting the Father/Master to
the test remains a constant activity, and one that gives rise to
an inner tug of war. On the one side there is the Law of the
Father, to which everything must be sacrificed including oneself. On the other side, this same law must be regularly evaded
and controlled for one's own sake. The result is a ceaseless
struggle that is displaced onto multiple objects of investment.
We find here the specific features of the obsessional personality that Freud summed up in the phrase *anal character*; consider,

for example, perseveration and obstinacy, the two privileged vehicles of obsessional investments.

It goes without saying that these traits derive their inexhaustible energy from the obsessional's attempt to achieve the control of *jouissance*, that is, the place of the father. Obsessionals are mighty conquerors in this respect, mobilizing the most insane and protracted means to win this fantasied mastery. But to no avail: no sooner is a goal reached than the obsessional sets out toward another one. Moreover, he is often quite offhand about turning away from what he has attained, giving it a good kick once he has mastered it.

In each of these "performances" the obsessional routinely fails to recognize that he is undergoing castration, which, for him, entails a return to the boundary that limits the illusion of totality, of achieving a global experience. This is why the conquests of the obsessional have so little appeal for him. What counts more is the new thing to be conquered, one further trophy in his endless ascent toward absolute control of *jouissance*. Obsessionals are champion climbers: the more forbidding and complex the path, the more they will go out of their way to make the journey.

The basic and persistent fantasy to which the obsessional clings is that of *jouissance* without lack, which he must attain at whatever cost. This clinging in turn illustrates the fantasy of the mouth that kisses itself (Freud 1905a). As Freud pointed out, the obsessional is an unrepentant mercenary engaged in an endless struggle to gain omnipotent control of the object. To this end he has at his disposal the full panoply of secondary gains from neurosis.

Another remarkable manifestation of obsessionality is found in the area of transgression. As we have seen, the obsessional feels constantly torn here on account of his ambivalence with regard to the Law of the Father. In his need to control the *jouis-*

sance of the object he inevitably comes up against transgression, and yet the weightiness of the law and the need to rely on it in order to escape the guilt of his unconscious libidinal impulses draw him into a conflict. In fact, it is quite rare for him to transgress in reality. He more often flirts with transgression in fantasy, where he can indulge it freely. One of the only areas in which actual transgression takes precedence over fantasy is that of sexual and romantic relationships, where it occurs in the form of acting out.

For the most part, however, the obsessional enacts transgression in the guise of its opposite. He makes a point of affecting a high degree of moral rigor, ostentatiously displaying unconditional adherence to laws and rules. He leaps to the defense of virtue and the soundness of established norms. His scrupulous concern for honesty in all matters can occasionally be carried to the point of folly: "Better to die than to yield an inch of ground!" This legalistic attitude, in which the obsessional skirts the edges of grandiosity and martyrdom, is of course inversely proportional to his unconscious desire to transgress.

If we consider saints to be the greatest experts on matters of *jouissance*, then obsessionals are the shabbiest moralists and the blindest zealots when it comes to the same issue. Their obstinacy in protecting order and virtue is equaled only by their total absence of discernment in knowing what it is they are protecting. Here is where we see the deployment of the most characteristic obsessional defenses. The essential task of isolation, for example, is to disconnect a thought, an attitude, or a behavior from its logical consequence. The psychic element isolated in this way from its context is at the same time deprived of its affect. The aim of this operation is to split off the affects of a representation linked to certain repressed contents. Stereotyped rituals and pauses in speech are the commonest signs of isolation, a systematic and radical defensive weapon that gives rise to the maintenance of self-control in all circumstances, even—and especially—in disasters. The apparent levelheadedness of obsessionals is nothing but this permanent control operating on the basis of isolation.

One of the most striking proofs of the tenacity of this process can be observed in the context of psychoanalytic treatment: the virtual disregard for the fundamental rule. The obsessional is blithely resistant to the process of free association that could circumvent his defensive isolation. In free association, the subject is asked to give up any attempt to exert control over his utterances and hence over the spontaneous emergence of any concomitant affects. The obsessional sees no alternative to resistance here, preferring to recite his material with frequent use of rationalization.

This defense is most clearly evident in one of the obsessional's favorite attitudes. He is an amazing investigator, a prodigious observer of the order of things and of the world, including himself insofar as he views himself objectively and abstractly as something apart from the surrounding environment. The subtlety and conscientiousness with which he deploys his keen observation are dependent on the isolation of affect. Furthermore, the obsessional's sense of humor, when it exists at all, stems from the deep compromise in which, in spite of everything, he knows he is actively involved, the compromise between split-off internalized affects and the need to express them somehow. This humor, which usually borders on derision, is thus a convenient way to discharge affects while still keeping watch over oneself. Thus the obsessional talks about himself from the position of this neutral observation point, making fun of that other who is himself.

He also makes use of another defense against affects, namely undoing. This mechanism allows him to take exception to a thought or an act and to behave as though it had never occurred. We have here an example of the constant concern for minimization so dear to obsessionals. Apart from the fact that the use of this defense reveals an enormous blindness, it also determines the kinds of humiliations to which obsessionals leave themselves open. Undoing is a compulsive process, one that is very effective in that it institutes a behavior that is the exact opposite of what the subject had originally undertaken. It affords the obsessional all sorts of secondary gains in terms of control and mastery.

As Freud often observed, undoing bears witness to one of the permanent conflicts with which the obsessional struggles, the archaic opposition between love and hate for an object of investment. For the most part it is hate that attempts to undo the element of love. What is going on here is a twofold process of investment and disinvestment typical of the obsessional's economy of desire; he flees his desire and undoes it as much as possible each time it is engaged authentically. In the next chapter we shall see how this dialectic is especially in evidence with regard to the obsessional's love objects.

18

The Obsessional and His Love Objects

When it comes to investment of love objects, the obsessional often gives his best, which, paradoxically, is both all and nothing at all—"all" in the sense that he can sacrifice everything, "nothing" in that he cannot accept loss. These are not two incompatible dispositions. On the contrary, they are the parameters within which the obsessional strategy of desire is stabilized.

This strategy revolves around the question of the other's *jouissance* and the obsessional's feeling that he has to be in total control of it, neutralizing all its outward signs. Therefore nothing must move, nothing must experience pleasure, and desire must be dead. Since the obsessional gives nothing in these circumstances, he loses nothing. But as soon as he observes the least external sign of *jouissance* in the other, he is prepared to sacrifice all and give all so that things may revert to their initial state.

If the problematic of loss, then, is so central in obsessional logic, this is because it refers directly to *lack*. To avoid confronting the question of lack, desire must somehow be overcome, since desire is precisely constituted and continually reopened as an issue by lack as such. The result is that desire, once it has been gagged, no longer lends itself to the articulation of even the smallest demand.

From this perspective we can understand why, given such a system of neutralization, the desired object is invested in a singular manner. It is assigned—indeed, consigned to—a position that is as far as possible that of a dead person. The obsessional constantly installs his love object in this place he finds so wonderful, a place where, in order to be loved and lovable, the object must play dead. Only in these circumstances does the obsessional's desiring machinery function at its best. If the other is "dead," he does not desire, and the obsessional can rest easy because desire is always desire of the other's desire. The permanent imperative that drives him in his love relationships depends on the other's not demanding anything, for, if the other demands, it is because he desires.

And so the obsessional mobilizes boundless energy in order that the other shall lack nothing and shall therefore not stir from his place. The universe of the other must thus remain scrupulously regimented, and it is through this total regimentation that the obsessional controls and masters the death of the desirous other. The discourse of the male obsessional abundantly confirms this murder: "She lacks nothing"; "She has everything she wants at home"; "She doesn't have to go to work"; and so on. Insofar as the obsessional seems to have to take care of everything, his feminine partner is satisfied in full and has nothing to demand. The object is thus presumed to be safe from all desire.

Such subjects in fact have an excessive inclination toward romantic imprisonment. They exert themselves unsparingly to create a first-class jail for the other. The embalming and mummification of the other must be achieved at all costs; the obsessional never holds back from such luxury because nothing can be too good as long as the loved one is honored in her abode of death. The other must accept her death; she would be ill-advised to express dissatisfaction with anything that has been done to bring her to that state. For the obsessional is very sensitive to the acknowledgment of the homage he pays to his romantic partner. The utmost, the height of, ingratitude would be for the partner not to be happy to be dead. In this situation, as in others, the obsessional is extremely preoccupied with justice. And what could be more unjust than for a woman to be ungrateful for the deadly concern that is meant to fulfill her completely?

Generally speaking, the obsessional strategy consists of appropriating a living object in order to turn it into a dead one and to see that it remains that way. For the most part, this is the precondition for his having loving relations with her. To attain this goal, he can also ennoble his object by making her ugly, that is, by transforming her into an object that is less and less desirable—which, in a way, guarantees her death. Moreover, this dethroning of her when it comes to desire has the additional advantage of securing imaginary ownership of the object in the face of the constant possibility that there may be a rival.

On this point we may note the prudishness of certain obsessionals toward their partners. This is always solidly rationalized by means of a whole series of didactic principles having to do with good taste and good manners in society. In this way some women are condemned never again to reveal the least part of their bodies outside of the rules of decorum. For certain obsessionals, such ideal norms involve constraining women in what amounts to armor-like clothing that reveals almost nothing. And should a rival cast even the briefest glance at this suit of armor, this only goes to prove that the woman is incorrigibly corrupt.

Not all obsessionals necessarily set out to make their love object undesirable. Some of them are keenly aware of the erotization of the other's body. This erotization, however, is tolerable only if the other is reduced to the level of an object, an object that can be displayed and whose brilliance can only reflect imaginarily on the owner. But here, even more than in any other situation, the object must then be completely extinguished, even radically dead. Only on this condition can it exist erotically. In a certain sense the erotic object serves the same function as a sports car, whose ideal role is to keep still so that its owner can be admired in it.

Other obsessionals pretend to have the same type of relationship with the equivalent of a feminine luxury automobile, but in the area of intellectual competition. There is a metonymic slide from the body of the car to its motor. This scenario involves an erotization of the brain of the intellectual, who has no right to exist unless she renounces forever any vague inclination toward physical sensuality.

In all these cases, the object is dead. But sooner or later the obsessional will inevitably have a crucial encounter with an object who refuses to continue playing this role; these dead objects tend to come back to life after all attempts to murder them. Such resurrections, however slight, unfailingly set off major cataclysms in the obsessional, who tastes the bitterness of childhood defeat. Just as there is nothing more reassuring and lovable than a female corpse, there is nothing more disturbing and hateful than a living woman, that is, one who can have pleasure. The obsessional can endure anything, neither keeping count nor sparing himself, with one exception, namely when the other experiences *jouissance* without him, without his being there or being involved in it. The other is not supposed to be able to take pleasure without his consent, his authorization. What is absolutely intolerable is for a woman to dare to challenge, in defiance of all established conventions, such a comfortable state of death—then the world turns upside down!

A corpse must not experience pleasure. A corpse with *jouissance* is all the more a traitor because if it takes pleasure it must desire. How can this be? It is so because, of necessity, each person's desire is always subject to the law of the other's desire, and that is just what the obsessional strives to remain unaware of.

In the life of the obsessional the fact of other's *jouissance* is always expressed in a certain agitation through which he tries to regain operational control. He is prepared to sacrifice all in order for things to return to the order of the death of desire. So that the other will once again be his object—a corpse without *jouissance*—he develops a boundless generosity, pays total homage, and undertakes all efforts and tasks. He engages in the most unexpected projects in order to win back the object, who, in escaping him, reminds him of loss.

In these strategies of recovery, incidentally, the obsessional can prove more hysterical than a true hysterical subject. He can offer a caricature of identifying with the object that he imagines to be that of the other's desire. It goes without saying that this slavishness usually has the opposite effect; the object is in no way won over and is even more alienated. His taking this servile tack only proves to her that the obsessional does not want to lose anything. The more he tries to be everything for the other, the more the obsessional indicates that he is nothing. What matters for the other is that a place be made for lack, for without lack desire cannot be sustained. The obsessional is therefore disqualified to the extent that he allows no room for lack and for what is owing to it in the dynamics of desire. All his masterful performances, his oaths of allegiance, and other covenants of good will are to no avail. The feminine partner is not deceived by all this, except when the obsessional's attempts to get back into her good graces happen to offer her the opportunity to derive secondary gains from her own personal neurosis. This is something we observe quite often in the case of some female hysterical partners. Thus one neurosis often summons up another in terms of a complementarity of symptoms.

References

Clavreul, J. (1981). *Le Désir et la Perversion*. Paris: Seuil.

Dor, J. (1985). *Introduction à la Lecture de Lacan*. Tome I: *L'inconscient Structuré Comme un Langage*. Paris: Denoël; English translation: *Introduction to the Reading of Lacan*, ed. J. Feher Gurewich, trans. S. Fairfield. Northvale, NJ: Jason Aronson, 1997.

——— (1987). *Structure et Perversions*. Paris: Denoël.

——— (1988). *L'A-scientificité de la Psychanalyse*. Tome I: *L'Aliénation de la Psychanalyse*. Tome II: *La Paradoxicalité Instauratrice*. Paris: Denoël.

——— (1989). *Le Père et sa Fonction en Psychanalyse*. Paris: Point Hors Ligne.

——— (1991). Manifestations perverses dans un cas de phobie. *Apertura* 5:95–100.

Freud, S. (1896). Further remarks on the neuro-psychoses of defence. *Standard Edition* 3:159–185.

——— (1900). The interpretation of dreams. *Standard Edition* 4–5.

——— (1905a). Three essays on the theory of sexuality. *Standard Edition* 7:125–243.

———— (1905b). Fragment of an analysis of a case of hysteria. *Standard Edition* 7:3–122.

———— (1908a). On the sexual theories of children. *Standard Edition* 9:207–226.

———— (1908b). Character and anal erotism. *Standard Edition* 9:169–175.

———— (1910). "Wild" psycho-analysis. *Standard Edition* 11:221–243.

———— (1911). Psycho-analytic notes on an autobiographical account of a case of paranoia (dementia paranoides). *Standard Edition* 12:3–79.

———— (1912). Recommendations to physicians practising psycho-analysis. *Standard Edition* 12:110–120.

———— (1913a). On beginning the treatment (further recommendations on the technique of psycho-analysis, I). *Standard Edition* 12:122–144.

———— (1913b). The disposition to obsessional neurosis: a contribution to the problem of choice of neurosis. *Standard Edition* 12:313–326.

———— (1915). Instincts and their vicissitudes. *Standard Edition* 14:111–140.

———— (1917a). On the transformations of instinct, as exemplified in anal erotism. *Standard Edition* 17:125–133.

———— (1917b). A difficulty on the path of psycho-analysis. *Standard Edition* 17:136–144.

———— (1920). Beyond the pleasure principle. *Standard Edition* 18:3–64.

———— (1921). Group psychology and the analysis of the ego. *Standard Edition* 18:67–143.

———— (1923). The infantile genital organization. *Standard Edition* 19:141–148.

———— (1924a). Neurosis and psychosis. *Standard Edition* 19:149–153.

————— (1924b). The loss of reality in neurosis and psychosis. *Standard Edition* 19:183–189.

————— (1927). Fetishism. *Standard Edition* 21:147–157.

————— (1938). Splitting of the ego in the process of defence. *Standard Edition* 23:271–277.

————— (1940). An outline of psycho-analysis. *Standard Edition* 23:141–207.

————— (1954). *The Origins of Psycho-analysis. Letters to Wilhelm Fliess, Drafts and Notes: 1887–1902*, ed. M. Bonaparte, A. Freud, and E. Kris, trans. E. Mosbacher and J. Strachey. New York: Basic Books.

Freud, S., and Breuer, J. (1895). Studies on hysteria. *Standard Edition* 2:1–305.

Hegel, G. W. F. (1807). *Phenomenology of Spirit*, trans. A. V. Miller. Oxford: Clarendon, 1985.

Jakobson, R. (1971). *Selected Writings*. The Hague: Mouton.

Krafft-Ebing, R. von (1899). *Psychopathia Sexualis*, trans. F. J. Rebman. London: Rebman.

Lacan, J. (1953). The function and field of speech and language in psychoanalysis. In Lacan 1977, pp. 30–113.

————— (1956). Situation de la psychanalyse et formation du psychanalyste en 1956. In *Écrits*, pp. 459–491. Paris: Seuil, 1966.

————— (1957). The agency of the letter in the unconscious or reason since Freud. In Lacan 1977, pp. 146–178.

————— (1957–58). *Les formations de l'inconscient*. Unpublished seminar.

————— (1977). *Écrits. A Selection*, trans. A. Sheridan. New York: Norton.

Laforgue, R. (1939). *Psychopathologie de l'échec*. Paris: Payot.

Laplanche, J., and Pontalis, J.-B. (1973). *The Language of Psychoanalysis*, trans. D. Nicholson-Smith. New York: Norton.

Mannoni, M. (1965). *Le Premier Rendez-vous avec le Psych-analyste.* Paris: Denoël/Gonthier.

Saussure, F. de (1916). *Course in General Linguistics,* ed. C. Bally and A. Sechehaye, trans. W. Baskin. Glasgow: Collins Fontana.

Schneiderman, S., ed. and trans. (1980). *Return to Freud: Clinical Psychoanalysis in the School of Lacan.* New Haven, CT: Yale University Press.

Index

Contributors

Joël Dor, psychoanalyst, is a Member of the Association de Formation Psychanalytique et de Recherches Freudiennes: Espace Analytique. He is in charge of lectures and is Director of Research in the Department of Training and Research in Clinical Human Sciences at the Université Denis-Diderot, Paris VII, where he teaches psychopathology and psychoanalysis. Widely published on the theory and practice of psychoanalysis, he is the author or co-author of several books forthcoming from Jason Aronson Inc.: *The Clinical Lacan, Structure and Perversion,* and *Lacanian Psychoanalysis: Theory and Practice.*

Judith Feher Gurewich, Ph.D., practices psychoanalysis in Cambridge, MA. She is affiliated with the Boston Psychoanalytic Institute and is a Member of the Association de Formation Psychoanalytique et de Recherches Freudiennes: Espace Analytique in Paris. Dr. Gurewich is the Director of the Lacan Seminar at Harvard University's Center for Literary and Cultural Studies. She has published a number of papers on various topics in psychoanalysis and the social sciences in French and American journals.

Susan Fairfield is an editor and translator of psychoanalytic books.